D1351162

So
You
Want
to
HUNT
GHOSTS?

© Jessica Labbé

About the Author

Deonna Kelli Sayed (Greensboro, NC) is a Muslim-American paranormal investigator with Haunted North Carolina (HNC). She lectures on many issues, from women in Islam to the paranormal, and has lived and conducted studies throughout Central Asia, the Middle East, Europe, and Africa. She is also the editor of Ghostvillage.com, the Internet's premier paranormal destination.

To Write to the Author

If you wish to contact the author or would like more information about this book, please write to the author in care of Llewellyn Worldwide, and we will forward your request. Both the author and publisher appreciate hearing from you and learning of your enjoyment of this book and how it has helped you. Llewellyn Worldwide cannot guarantee that every letter written to the author can be answered, but all will be forwarded. Please write to:

Deonna Kelli Sayed
⁒ Llewellyn Worldwide
2143 Wooddale Drive
Woodbury, MN 55125-2989

Please enclose a self-addressed stamped envelope for reply,
or $1.00 to cover costs. If outside the USA, enclose
an international postal reply coupon.

So
You
Want
to
HUNT
GHOSTS?

A Down-to-Earth Guide

DEONNA KELLI SAYED

Llewellyn Publications
Woodbury, Minnesota

FIRST EDITION
First Printing, 2012

Editing by Laura Graves
Book design by Bob Gaul
Cover art: Background image © iStockphoto.com/ShutterWorx
Cover design by Kevin R. Brown

Llewellyn is a registered trademark of Llewellyn Worldwide Ltd.

Library of Congress Cataloging-in-Publication Data
Sayed, Deonna Kelli.
  So you want to hunt ghosts?: a down-to-earth guide/Deonna Kelli Sayed.—1st ed.
      p. cm.
  Includes bibliographical references (p.   ) and index.
  ISBN 978-0-7387-3125-4
1. Ghosts. 2. Parapsychology—Investigation. I. Title.
  BF1471.S19 2012
  133.1—dc23
                          2012020797

Llewellyn Publications
A Division of Llewellyn Worldwide Ltd.
2143 Wooddale Drive
Woodbury, MN 55125-2989
www.llewellyn.com

Printed in the United States of America

Contents

Acknowledgments

There is a long list of people to thank for this book. I am forever grateful for Troy Taylor, Dr. Barry Taff, and Loyd Auerbach's support and vision. I thank Jim Hall and Steve Barrell from Haunted North Carolina for keeping the way lit with hope and enthusiasm. I am deeply grateful to Marie D. Jones for her girl support. David Rountree and Paul Browning are innovative inspirations. The AdventureMyths crew—I am humbled and awed by your support. I thank Jeff Belanger for putting me in my place and for always insisting that everyone is part of the story. Michelle Belanger (no relation to Jeff) remains the smartest person I know. Michael Robartes, you are kind and wonderful to tolerate my constant emails. I forgive you for walking away from me during that first conversation. I also want to thank my editor, Amy Glaser, and my agent, Lisa Hagan, for their continued support.

I give a special recognition to Valerie Robbins, Assistant Director of the International Paranormal Reporting Group's Eastern Oregon Team, for her donation to the Hasbro Children's Hospital during the 2011 TAPS Family Reunion.

Finally, I reserve a special shout-out for the Green Bean Coffee House in downtown Greensboro. The staff gifted me sanctuary while writing this book. I am forever grateful for their morning Red Eye and equally sorry that they have no resident ghosts.

Introduction

My start on the ghost-hunting trek was like many others'. If you are like me, you are most likely a product of paranormal reality TV. The shows have become a cultural force opening an unprecedented space to publicly discuss hauntings, psychic abilities, and supernatural experiences of all sorts.

Television aside, many people who adopt the ghost-hunter moniker discover this to be an amazing journey of personal transformation. Most of us start small and then find this interest becoming an increasingly larger part of our lives. No matter what approach you take—that of a casual observer or a serious researcher—there is no shame in being part of this avocation. And I suspect that many of us move beyond the TV experience at some point to engage with the larger history of psychical research, occult studies, and parapsychology in efforts to better understand the phenomena at hand.

I was lucky enough to be close to a few good groups, including Haunted North Carolina, which is close to (but not affiliated with) the

Rhine Research Center, the former Duke Parapsychology Lab. I met the right people and obtained a diverse yet (hopefully) solid education about the paranormal field. Of course, my knowledge extended beyond the TV screen, which is ultimately very limited in scope and representation. Even paranormal reality TV cast members will tell you that TV provides a very small picture of all that is involved in real investigation!

Many may not realize how much research occurred prior to reality TV. What I want readers to come away with is an appreciation for the vast nature of this research and the personalities behind many assumptions most of us take out on investigation.

At some point, I quickly realized there was so much I did not know about paranormal investigation, and most of it I would never learn from a TV show. I began reading wonderful books by longtime researchers such as Troy Taylor, Loyd Auerbach, Joshua Warren, Hans Holzer, Rosemary Ellen Guiley, and others. These authors have produced amazing works reflecting the long history and multiple approaches to seeking the unknown. Most of these books were written prior to the earth sized shift in the culture of ghost hunting that occurred with paranormal reality TV.

An unprecedented number of people have taken up the cause. The shows have altered the way people discuss paranormal activity and have forever changed the landscape of paranormal investigation. A wave of technical innovation has swept the field with experimental equipment (of varying degrees of credibility) and new investigative techniques. Most importantly, a unique ethical reality is emerging as more people than ever are opening up their homes to a growing number of paranormal investigators. There are now potential legal, privacy, and liability issues that did not exist a few years ago.

I realized there was no book that really looked at these contemporary issues (although the authors of the previous books are very involved in current discussions), so I decided to take up the cause. In the past, books about ghost hunting were directed at specific—and normally discreet—individuals who were into this sort of thing. The books were important how-to manuals. For better or worse, TV and the subsequent blossoming paranormal culture have lessened the learning curve. Being a ghost hunter today is a distinct social marker immediately recognizable to the larger public.

The game has changed. Paranormal groups are expected to have a high level of organization to function efficiently. Furthermore, ethical paranormal investigation requires solid case management, running a reputable group, and responsible evidence presentation. At the same time, observers suggest that the growth of group culture may actually impede real research: it limits who can investigate and stifles access to haunted public sites. I explore these elements in the book.

There are competing philosophies in paranormal investigation. Some want to help clients with troubling situations or assist curious homeowners understand unexplained events. There are some investigators who also feel called to assist the spirits. Likewise, a growing number of investigators want to take a more scientific approach and do controlled research to uncover whatever processes are at play during paranormal phenomena. Finally, a very large demographic is interested in *legend tripping*—just having a cool experience. This may not involve science or helping people, but it does serve up a healthy dose of learning local history and folklore. All types of exploration are important even if they are sometimes competing against one another in the larger picture.

Good investigators also honor history, and historical research is one of the golden nuggets paranormal investigators offer the world. Some teams have uncovered amazing historical facts that turn out to be more intriguing than any ghostly evidence! Yet, few books really get into the specifics of how to conduct historical research. It isn't as basic as "going to the court house"—although one may have to do that.

In the past, a reputable psychic or medium was part and parcel of investigation. Some teams have ditched the role of psychic ability in favor of a purely technical and equipment-oriented approach. There are advantages to this: today, there are too many psychics to shake a stick at and often it is difficult to gauge credibility. At the same time, equipment leaves out an element of human consciousness, and this variable may be an essential component in understanding and experiencing the paranormal. I look at the role of consciousness, sometimes referred to as "psi" in certain circles, as well as the importance of technological equipment. Regardless of how one feels about psychics, everybody seems to be impressed with equipment—but many often have little knowledge about how to properly use the various devices in the field.

I also take care to explore debates around devices that are becoming more popular on investigation, such as Instrumental Transcommunication Devices (ITCs). Some consider these highly controversial items to be amazing assets in an investigator's toolbox. However, ITCs are ethically problematic even if they seem to be the future of paranormal investigation.

It is also increasingly necessary for anyone who calls him- or herself a "ghost hunter" or "paranormal investigator" to examine why they are doing this. It is also essential for investigators to understand what they believe about the paranormal. No book really explores these issues, from group management to ethical behavior to the role of personal philosophy. This is a great resource for beginners as well as for seasoned investigators who want to take it up a notch.

I consider myself a fortunate newcomer to this business, so I purposely engaged those who have been around far longer to share their own insights. This book is a type of encyclopedia of ghost hunting and provides one way (but by no means the only way) to investigate ghostly phenomena.

This book is not an overly technical manual. There are other seminal works that explain in profound detail how to work with EMF meters and provide more hands-on aspects of equipment use. Some are written by authors I discuss here: Troy Taylor, Joshua Warren, Loyd Auerbach, David Rountree, and Christopher Balzano. Their books are excellent and, dare I say, almost required reading for any paranormal investigator. *So You Want to Hunt Ghosts* touches on the basics but focuses more on how to manage a group, cases, and research design, and it provides some discussion on emerging ethics. It is not meant to replace any how-to books; instead, it provides a fleshed-out discussion about the new dynamics and issues facing paranormal investigators.

What I want any reader to take from this book is an appreciation for the multiple approaches involved in paranormal research, as well as the long legacy that existed prior to reality TV. Finally, the first component in any investigation is to understand the philosophies and motivations behind the work. This book is not a technical manual but an overview of these issues that affect all aspects of paranormal investigation.

1: Basic Concepts

What are Ghosts, Anyway?

My very first experiences with the unexplained began in my childhood bedroom. I suppose that is where all good ghost stories start.

I lived in a fairly new brick home on a dirt road in rural north Florida. I was about six years old. It was a dark and stormy night. I saw a reflection in the mirror—a black figure with two glowing eyes that stood in the doorway. If that wasn't clichéd enough, what I remember most about the event is that I felt its presence before I saw it. In fact, the sensation that *something was there* was more significant than the sighting! I certainly do not claim to be psychic, but that event marked the beginning of sensing and experiencing things for years in my childhood home.

That early moment help me appreciate the role of personal experience when it comes to ghosts. What we know about paranormal events really begins with the stories people tell. In reality, most ghostly events are about the living. As Loyd Auerbach writes, "People experience these things, people report them, and people need help with them."

But what *are* these things? What does it mean to have a ghost or for something to be haunted? I have conducted several surveys among paranormal investigators and it is unclear what a "ghost" is in the first place. For anyone interested in paranormal investigation or even legend tripping (going out and engaging story of folklore or just having a good time), it is essential to really think about we are actually seeking.

Most people use the term "ghost" to explain anything odd and vaguely creepy, from rapping noises to shadow figures to full-bodied apparitions. Those events all make great stories. From a research perspective, however, the term "ghosts" needs to be fleshed out (pun intended).

Ghosts, Hauntings, and Apparitions

The ghost question is a hefty one. There are endless varieties of ghost stories just as there are hypotheses and ideas about why they exist. It really depends on whom you ask about ghosts—and I suppose at what point in history you do the asking.

There is no other concept that carries such religious, spiritual, and scientific weight. Despite the current popularity of paranormal reality TV, several polls indicate that only about half of Americans believe in ghosts (or admit to a belief). The other way of looking at it, I suppose, is that only half of Americans at any one time approve of whatever president is the White House. That puts things in perspective a bit.

Ghosts are as contentious as politics. For many, spirited activity is very real. The majority of Americans may not say they believe in ghosts, but it seems everyone has a story. Paranormal investigators live for these stories. We want to poke, prod, and embrace stories of all sorts. What we believe about these accounts determines what we do with them.

People have been poking with the paranormal forever. The first time any human asked a "big question" about god or the nature of reality was an early attempt at understanding the unseen. In reality, the metaphysical realm has determined cultural and belief systems from the minute language entered the picture—and that was a long, long time ago!

Ancient wisdom is an important window into current phenomena, perhaps, but I want to inform readers about contemporary personalities who have affected what you and I believe about ghosts. So what better way to start than to review their contributions?

Joshua Warren, author of *How to Hunt Ghosts: A Practical Guide*, suggests that ghosts, apparitions, haints, and specters are "some paranormal aspect of the physical form and/or mental presence that appears to exist apart from the original physical form." Fair enough; it is something that is not contained in a corporal body. This perspective sums up what many believe to be a ghost or spirit. He also believes activity may be attributed to imprints, warps, poltergeists, and naturals (or earth spirits).

Loyd Auerbach, a well-respected parapsychologist, points out that the term "ghost" is used to refer to a "form of a person after he or she has died," but that definition can extend to even animal spirits or phantom noises. Auerbach fleshes out a parapsychology point of view, which distinguishes between a ghost and an apparition.

Among lay ghost hunters, the term "apparition" normally refers to some type of figure of a deceased person (or pet) witnessed by an observer. However, that description is not very specific. Auerbach refers to an apparition as "the concept of human personality or consciousness (or that of an animal) appearing in some form after death." In a traditional sense, apparitions refer to intelligent spirits that have an ability to interact with the living. This does not mean they necessarily appear in physical form. Apparitions are intelligent, disembodied consciousness that can interact with you and me.

Here is where terminology gets interesting. Many people remember early *Ghost Hunters* seasons with Jason Hawes arguing about when to label a location as haunted or merely designating it as paranormally active. It seemed like a big deal for something to earn the "haunted" label, and many investigators developed a cultlike mentality around the word. It was never clear, at least to me, what made something definitively haunted for Hawes.

Parapsychologists sorted this out a long time ago. Hauntings, unlike apparitions, are recordings (residual haunted, imprints, or place memory). These are the footsteps one hears every Thursday at 3 a.m., or the floating specter that roams the same path on a certain date every year.

Troy Taylor is credited for coining the term "residual haunt" although the idea of the environment recording and replaying activity is an ancient concept. He postulates that it is difficult to really classify certain types of hauntings. However, he suggests that the traditional, intelligent-type haunting may not be as popular and common as many people believe. For Taylor, intelligent haunts "will manifest in physical ways in an attempt to interact with those at the location," such as slamming doors and cold spots. The observer may or may not impact how the events materialize.

According to Taylor, the most common type of activity is the residual haunt, or "place memory" (parapsychologists) or imprints (as discussed by Joshua Warren). Place memory may involve geologic and environmental components including (but not limited to) atmospheric conditions, static electricity, moon phases, geomagnetism, and even building materials that serve as "stone tape" recorders. Taylor extrapolates to suggest that water serves as a powerful conductor for place memory, particularly underground water sources. There may be an environmental component to this. Taylor references studies conducted by the scientists in a nonparanormal-related field suggesting that water has a type of "memory." He theorizes that at some point, residual haunts will fade away as energy is depleted. While an interactive ghost is deemed the most interesting, residual cases are most likely the primary source of most ghost stories.

One of the most significant philosophical divides when it comes to ghosts and hauntings is what role the *living* play in the actual activity. Auerbach makes an important distinction here that is key to what many investigators do not consider: a *living agent* is needed to receive the haunting, meaning that our own telepathy is at work at some level in experiencing even residual haunts. For Auerbach, this suggests "hauntings actually show that we are all psychic receivers to some degree." Not everyone experiences apparitions and hauntings in the same manner. Some will sense a spirit, others may actually see it, some may hear it speak, while others may sniff phantom smells or feel cold spots. As such a concept requires a vastly different philosophical and methodological approach, I will look at this variable a bit later.

Hans Holzer is another significant contributor to how we understand the paranormal; he coined the phrase "the other side." There are few investigators who have compiled such detailed case studies for the general public. Holzer was interesting in his perspectives. He was specific in his terminology, distinguishing between ghosts and spirits. For Holzer, ghosts are "individuals unaware of their own passing or incapable of accepting the transition because of unfinished business." How one becomes a ghost depends on a person's attitude or emotional state at the time of death. Ghosts are incapable of profound intellectual processes and are therefore limited in scope and personality. These ghosts are almost like personality remnants.

Spirits, for Holzer, are different than ghosts. These specters have moved on to the next realm yet have emotional ties to living people or places. Unlike ghosts, spirits have fuller capabilities to interact. Furthermore, he did not believe that spirits could travel from place to place, suggesting that they were location-based. That idea is contested in today's paranormal community with many believing in spirit attachments or the need for protection while on investigation. Holzer's works provide examples of thorough ways to document a case and explore everything from haunted locations to spirit attachments. He also had one foot in parapsychology and discussed psychic impressions. He used *trance mediums* on cases—something rarely seen among the contemporary investigators. Holzer also believed in place memory and was influenced by esoteric aspects, Spiritualism, and the more scientific approaches of parapsychology. Author Marie D. Jones sums up Holzer's approach as someone who "believes that ghosts are trapped in a state between two worlds" because of unfinished business. Many investigators today agree with these sentiments.

Something to Know:

Trance Medium is a term referring to someone with specific psychical abilities to physically channel sentient energies. Those who are trance mediums go into a type of literal trance or altered state, and may exhibit body language, accents, and mannerisms of whatever ghost or spirit they are in communication with. Not all mediums are trance mediums.

As you can see, there are different philosophies and approaches from contemporary thinkers even when based upon several decades of academic psychical research. Some feel that ghosts are some type of energy trapped in our world, while others feel that this energy may come from another dimension. Some hypotheses require the living as a filter. Many investigators believe that ghosts are actual souls or personalities of the dead. Certain people are invested in the concept that a traumatic incident or unfinished businesses causes souls to linger or that the environment can somehow record such events. You may believe all of the above and whatever you feel to be true will affect how you might investigate. Even approaching something "objectively" or as a skeptic is a belief system.

We will later go into case studies or more detailed discussion on some these concepts. But let us now look at a few more variables some feel are related to ghosts and hauntings.

Portals

I have a close relationship with a haunted historic home in North Carolina called Körner's Folly. This whimsical home, built in 1878, is considered to be America's Strangest House due to its unique architectural and interior design courtesy of the builder, Jule Körner. What is strange about this lovely historic site is the resident spirits. During numerous investigations, teams have captured strong EVP of children, as well as interactive male and female entities.

Körner's Folly offers a unique investigative opportunity in numerous ways. The location seems to be a happy haunt as it was a happy home. Another interesting research perspective is that 80 percent of the home's furnishings are original and designed by Mr. Körner. Many investigators postulate that objects may be haunted or serve as a way for a spirit to attach itself to this world. I cannot say if these original furnishings play a role in whatever paranormal activity is in the house. There was a short time the home served as funeral parlor and there are rumors that employees used to open up in the morning to find the furniture rearranged. As Jule Körner was a furniture designer, there may be some credence to these reports!

While Körner's Folly has spirited activity and unique decorative items, I was particularly floored one day to find out one local team thought they had located an onsite portal.

The team came to investigate, and I saw their evidence—all eight pages and ten orb photos worth of it. In one photo, the team claimed to have captured a vortex. The camera was tilted sideways and there was a swirly thing going on.

To make a long story short and pitiful, it took an email or two to confirm my suspicion: this was a badly digitally altered attempt that made a laughingstock of this team. There were no portals in Körner's Folly, and if there were, it probably would not show up so neatly swirled.

Despite the badly faked photo, the concept resonates among many investigators who do believe in portals, a fringe idea to some yet highly endorsed by others. Troy Taylor writes extensively about portals as he does believe in the concept. For enthusiasts, portals may explain additional phenomena, from UFOs to crypto sightings.

The idea is related to historically sacred spaces or locations with a long history of strange activity. There is a hypothesis of a correlation with magnetic lines that run beneath the earth. Alfred Watkins originally suggested the "ley line" idea in 1925 which suggests that many sacred sites are connected via an earth energy path. For Watkins, these events occur at places where ley lines intersect. This idea no longer carries scientific resonance but still remains an intriguing one for many.

Taylor suggests that some cemeteries may be portals. There are divisive opinions about cemeteries, as pointed out in this book. Just because dead bodies are buried somewhere does not make a place haunted. Some believe that unmarked, mass, or desecrated burial sites may be a source of paranormal accounts. Of course, some cemeteries are linked to homesteads or other historical events that may replay as a haunting. But some cemeteries do appear to have intelligent paranormal activity, so what gives?

For Taylor, one theory may be that such places are crossing-over sights. He suggests that some burial locations sprang up because people may have sensed these locations were somehow spiritually significant. Taylor also feels there may be other portals as well, including some that may reveal frightening or unusual apparitions or images that may not appear human. I do not get too deeply into concepts of earth spirits or elementals in this book, although a few ghost-hunting teams claim to have cases dealing with such.

Regardless if one believes in portals or vortices, the concept is cross cultural and appears in folklore around the world. It appears in the language some use to discuss paranormal activity. Intriguingly, science may ultimately provide an explanation that transcends folklore.

I bring up portals not because I am an advocate but because there is some overlap in the concept with quantum physics and the holographic theory of the universe, which I explore a little later.

Marie D. Jones is a personal friend as well as an author who writes extensively about related subjects. I asked her what the whole portal business is about. She responded, "I think they are like wormholes or breaches in time and space which allow for a bleed-through. They don't necessarily have to be wormholes in the traditional black hole/white hole sense. They can be land-based portals where perhaps because of resonant frequency synchronization or other environmental factors, the veil between worlds or realities is thin or opened for a short period of time … this would explain paranormal and UFO hot spots." She goes on to explain how language may muddle the concept: "When people see the word 'portal' they think of the sci-fi image of a gateway or stargate, but that is just a visual image of the concept of a breach or opening between two dimensions, two realities, two universes." She points out that photos of so-called vortices or portals may not be as strong evidence of these phenomena as historical and ongoing accounts.

Something to Know:

Some investigators will label something a "portal" haunting without any real evidence to back it up. The portal concept becomes a free-for-all or one-stop explanation for whatever activity is occurring. Before one jumps on the vortex bandwagon, it is best to have a long history of documented accounts or some other strong evidence supporting a portal claim.

Demons and Other Inhumans

Many investigators today strongly believe in negative entities, meaning beings that have never walked the earth in human form. This is a highly divisive concept. In many ways, the idea of negative haunts is at the core of larger philosophical debates about ghosts and hauntings, for it bucks science in favor of a purely spiritual approach to the paranormal.

The concept of demons is that they are real beings able to affect our everyday world—they are mentioned in the Bible, for example. One mainstream reverend I know commented that people readily believe in the Holy Spirit and angels but seem to disavow the existence of demons. After all, the Bible clearly states that Jesus cast demons out of people.

Some paranormal investigators are absolutely convinced that demons are real and can possess and oppress the living. The root of this approach is that humanity caught in the middle of a war between God and Satan. The Catholic Church has official exorcists. Likewise, many Protestant denominations also have clergy who perform exorcisms or blessings, albeit quietly. Still, some Christians often have a hard time getting clergy to take their seemingly mundane paranormal concerns seriously.

There is darkness in the world. Just look at the behavior of the living to affirm that meanness exists. Why and how darkness is experienced paranormally is still up for discussion.

Many arguments abound regarding what makes a case demonic. Religious conservative types suggest that everything paranormal is demonically related, but that idea has lessened in popularity over the years. Those who do believe in demons suggest that true cases are very rare yet very real indeed. What is certain is that demonic hauntings are considered distinct in their characteristics.

Keith Johnson is a well-known investigator having been with TAPS on *Ghost Hunter* episodes and *Paranormal State*. Keith and his wife Sandra are wonderful, credible people. He suggests that demonic cases have several telltale signs: demons seem to be resentful of humanity, often attack by making someone fearful, and can leave physical marks such as welts and bites. There may be foul odors and low, guttural growls associated with demonic cases. There is often a "fight or flight" response among those familiar with such infestations.

Other concepts point to other inhumans, such as elementals and faeries, as the source for hauntings. Rosemary Ellen Guiley's work explores these topics as well as some of Barry Fitzgerald's writings. It is unclear for me as a researcher how one can systematically research such claims in the same manner that we do ghosts and hauntings and it also seems few investigators in the United State receive earth spirit cases.

As a Muslim person, I have researched stories around the *djinn* as well. I personally find this concept to be intriguing. Djinn are thought to be interdimensional beings created prior to humankind. They have free will, unlike demons, and can be naughty or nice. In the Muslim world, djinn are associated with all types of paranormal activity. While I do not believe that to be the case, they may provide a source of some activity that is labeled as demonic AND as run-of-the mill paranormal stuff.

The Djinn are thought to be able to possess, and the symptoms are similar to what is believed to be demonic possession: extraordinary strength, speaking in foreign languages, having two voices come out of one body. There is a cottage industry of exorcists throughout the Muslim world.

....

Something to Know:

The djinn are mentioned in the Qu'ran and thought to predate humanity as interdimensional beings with free will. They provide a conceptual framework to explain some paranormal events, perhaps shadow people, that seem to fall outside of intelligent spirits and demonics—as something that is interactive, intelligent, but not necessarily or inherently evil. There are differing opinions regarding the nature of the djinn, however. Thanks to the work of Rosemary Ellen Guiley and Phil Imbrogno, the djinn concept is becoming better known in the paranormal community.

....

There are cases that baffle any rational explanation. There are also cases where you can almost "sense" a type of negativity the minute you enter the property. I am certainly not one to throw the demon card out, but I have been in circumstances where my skin was crawling with "not so nice" vibes. Indeed, I understand why many people say that darker cases elicit a "flight or fight" response.

Religious rhetoric forms the worldview of many ghost hunters. It is interesting, however, that few in the field attribute happy or pleasant haunts to angelic entities. In all my time as a paranormal investigator, I have yet to come across someone who thinks angels are the ones moving things in the house! As such, I moved angels out of the research equation—until a family member shared an interesting story.

A few years ago, my cousin was hospitalized in the Intensive Care Unit due to a serious undiagnosed health problem. While in the ICU, he was in and out of consciousness and under heavy sedation for several days.

Despite his mental state, he clearly remembers an Asian nurse coming in to care for him on numerous occasions. She not only attended to him but she also spoke with him about very specific, personal events in his life—private information he was shocked to hear her reveal. He was unable to speak during this time but tried to acknowledge his gratitude through slight body motions.

She was attending him one day when a pair of nurses entered the room. At that point, his Asian nurse said, "Oh, I have to go now," and promptly disappeared. He did not see her exit through the one door into the room, and that was also the last time her saw her.

He immediately improved and was able to speak a few days later. At this point, my cousin wanted to specifically nominate this woman for a special acknowledgement program the hospital had in place. He had no reason to believe that she wasn't flesh and blood and started asking staff about the "Asian nurse."

No one knew whom he was referring to. This is a rural area with few Asian people and certainly, even fewer Asian nurses.

However, two nurses came in one day and he attempted one more time to inquire about this woman. Nurse One started indicated that she had no idea regarding the person's identity. Nurse Two promptly shushed her and kindly (yet cryptically) said, "Yes, we have heard of her. Other patients have *seen* her and she is a very, very good nurse."

The conversation ended there. My cousin realized that he had not experienced a real person. He had encountered what he felt was his guardian angel, who spiritually nursed him back to health.

Despite his assessment, my first inclination is that my cousin witnessed a resident hospital ghost who comforts those in need, particularly if Nurse Two was telling the truth about other patients having the same experiences. In my cousin's worldview, however, he encountered an angel. This idea gave him a great deal of comfort.

We may never know what really went down but this provides a wonderful example how personal belief determines the retelling of the story!

Angels aside, most cultures express beliefs in a dark unseen, and like angels, such concepts also filter into our language through folklore and religion. Regardless of what one believes, it is important to consider both spirit and science when approaching such cases.

Another type of inhuman case revolves around earth spirits or elements, first discussed in the section on portals. I find these reports intriguing, as they seem to rarely occur despite accounts of "wee people" in cultures around the world.

....

Something to Know:

Earth spirits or elementals refer to sentient beings that walk the earth yet are not (and have never been) human. They are sometimes also referred to as the wee people, fairies (the fae), or gnomes. Cultures around the world represent these concepts in a variety of ways. These beings are tied to nature and are not necessarily evil although they may be mischievous. Some believe elementals are separate beings that can be controlled through occult activity. Most contemporary investigators do not express a great deal of research interest or have case reports dealing with these beings, although there are a few exceptions.

....

Coincidentally, I stumbled across a potential elemental case while writing this book. A friend in the Pacific Northwest who is a credible journalist is a paranormal investigator in his spare time. He shared with me what he feels was an elemental experience in a private home.

He received a case report from a middle-aged single woman, a devout Christian who felt she was being watched. There were reports of objects moving in her home. My friend went to the house and noted nothing unusual in terms of EMF or any naturally occurring variables that would cause paranoia. The client seemed of sound mind yet concerned.

He spent a few hours on site conducting EVP work that resulted in no evidence. However, he noted that he felt "off" during his time there. He described it as a type of energy buzz that one sometimes feels in active locations, but he had nothing except a "feeling" to go on. My friend had asked the client if she could mark an event or instance that seemed to trigger the activity—perhaps small home renovations or any emotional occurrences in her life. She could not pinpoint anything specific at the time.

The lady called a few days later. It was evening and she was out in her car scared to death, wanting him to come right away. She said activity at night had worsened and that she was now experiencing "little beings with pointy ears standing outside of her windows and laughing at her." It certainly sounded odd and fantastical. Yet this woman was very scared to stay in her home in the evenings, and the activity seemed to be escalating. He had no reason to believe that she was delusional or suffering from mental health issues.

He returned to the home and proceeded to investigate. Once again, he asked her if she remembered anything that could have served as a trigger. She then made an off comment about having some tree stumps removed from the yard and then immediately realized that the activity had started right after that.

Bingo, thought my friend, *this may be an elemental case.* In his area of the Pacific Northwest, particularly in rural areas, he estimates teams encounter elemental-type behavior at least 10 percent of the time. He surmised the tree stump removal had upset whatever resident earth spirits inhabited the yard.

He explained to the client the earth spirit concept and suggested that she put a pot of vinegar and black pepper outside of her doors and windows. He said this is believed to keep elementals at bay. Later, he also recommended she walk through her house banging pots and pans around and "staking her ground" by telling the spirits that this was her home and they had to leave. He made this suggestion as it is thought elementals dislike loud noises.

My friend also recommended that she bring a priest in to bless her home, something that was in line with her personal beliefs. He took great care to explain that the beings were not demonic at all but a normal, earthy (if not mischievous) part of our unseen world. However, the intent of the living—in this case, the woman—is sometimes a variable, and operating within ones own personal faith system has a great deal of power. As a follow-up note, activity decreased after she put out the vinegar and staked her private space with the banging of metal. However, it was not until she had the home blessed that activity completely stopped.

Was this an actual elemental case? It is hard to say for sure but it provides intriguing food for thought. As a side note, I know some Instrumental Transcommunication researchers (ITCs in this case being ghost and spirit boxes) claim to have nondemonic inhumans come through occasionally.

I now move from the spirit (literally) to the flesh—that of the living—to explore some variables associated with paranormal research that many contemporary investigators know little about.

Poltergeist Activity (or Psychokinesis)

Another component of ghost hunting—and one that is marginalized, as many are just out for a "ghostly" experience—is the poltergeist case. For parapsychologists, the term "poltergeist" does not refer to a noisy ghost but a living agent, meaning a person in the environment who is the agent for psychokinesis, or PK. Loyd Auerbach debunks the prevalent theory that only young girls serve as agents. There are plenty of documented cases where people of all ages are PK agents. Things move around. Weird events happen when certain individuals are present, and this normally reflects some inner emotional turmoil or stress that has no other way of relieving itself.

Taylor also believes that poltergeist activity can be related to a living agent, but an intelligent haunt may also be the source. I have run into many investigators who feel a poltergeist agent may also "attract" spirits, thus increasing paranormal activity in their surroundings. Loyd Auerbach states that individuals with PK abilities may serve as a type of amplifier for residual and intelligent energies. A home may be dormant for years until someone with unknown PK talents moves in.

Poltergeist cases are normally defined by their temporary duration (activity decreases over time), the presence of moving objects, and a perceived living agent. Some people who are agents, or living with agents, may feel they are being attacked or oppressed by a spirit or negative entity. A little information about PK can go a long way and be just as interesting as a ghost!

I personally have had two possible poltergeist-type experiences in my life. Both occurred during extraordinary emotional times during which I experienced a type of stress I envisioned to be suppressed within my chest. The emotions were "boxed in" to stop me from having a complete meltdown. The situations surrounding these stresses remain personal. Yet these are the only two times I experienced such profound, compacted anxiety.

The first incident resulted in a light bulb completely shattering near the face of someone towards whom I held deep resentment. The other incident involved me feeling compelled to look at a smoke alarm in my home, only to have it immediately go off as soon as I glanced up. It was 2:20 am. I was alone, deeply stressed, and in tremendous physical pain from outpatient surgery I'd had earlier in the day. I was not in the mood to climb up to turn the thing off, but I had to.

The point of this story is this: I immediately sensed that this was PK rather than a ghost, demon, or negative attachment. I understood what was going on and realized I needed to somehow work through the stress. Are these true cases of PK? I have no idea. But I do know that these events correlated with some of the most profound emotional turmoil I've ever experienced, one apparent prerequisite for some PK activity.

I've also had cases that seemed to involve apparitional (intelligent haunts) but also living agent PK. In 2011, Haunted North Carolina inherited a case featured on *Ghost Hunters*. In this residential home, there were EVP, shadow figures, and several witnesses to a variety of activity. The eldest child, age four, claimed to interact with a kind spirit named "Bringy."

There were also reports of things moving in the kitchen. Or to be more precise, objects also being thrown *from* the kitchen into the living room. One particular incident involved a wedding ring flying off of a coffeepot. I asked the client if she and her husband were arguing at the time. Indeed, they were having what she described as a "minor disagreement" about a longstanding issue in the marriage.

Some of this activity was almost textbook PK. This was a military family with a husband in the Special Forces. The wife had delivered three children in a period of five years and was often alone while her husband was abroad to parts unknown. She admitted to having little support and no nearby family. This client is one of the calmest, sweetest women I have encountered. I was truly baffled (and inspired) by her serene demeanor. Valium would be my best friend if I had her stress level!

Our team understood that PK was one potential variable in this situation. We conducted a simple experiment with the expectation that absolutely nothing would come out of it. The client had a necklace with a small pendant. We hung that from the ceiling fan light chain and waited until all air circulation stopped and the necklace was still.

The client was instructed to stare at the necklace and envision a mental muscle moving it. No throbbing blood vessels were involved—this wasn't an X-Men competition. We asked her to concentrate on the necklace until we told her to stop. While doing so, we immediately distracted her with questions about her children. Meanwhile, the video recorder remained focused on the necklace. After a few minutes of casual conversations, we reviewed the footage.

Over a period of a few minutes, the necklace slowly began to move to the right. Well, to be more specific, it started to *hover* to the right. It was not swaying or swirling around, but literally hovering at what was a measurable angle. We held a pen up to the video to gauge measurement and watched as the necklace slowly shifted. I was baffled and completely surprised that this happened at all, especially on the first try!

I later asked HNC's director, Jim Hall, if maybe one of us might have PK abilities that moved the necklace. He suggested that a group effort could be a variable, but it demonstrated to the client that PK was one possibility.

We reviewed past claims with the client. She noticed that case claims involving moving objects occurred during times of extreme personal stress, which for her was most often when her husband was deployed. Likewise, most incidents occurred during pregnancy—massive hormonal shifts. Her eyes lit up as we pieced these puzzles together.

"Oh my God," she commented. "I see the patterns now! This all makes sense!"

Jason and Grant suggested that her home had residual activity. With Auerbach's ideas in place, we postulated that her PK may be almost like an amplifier for some of the residual activity. This made sense to her.

We may not have figured out all the elements in this particular case, but it was nice to link some activity to PK. It was also intriguing to consider how this affected other experiences in the home. This is an ongoing case for us but it was empowering to have a client so excited when we applied the PK theory. Sometimes thinking outside of the ghost box can do wonders.

Dr. William Roll has extensively studied PK, and his work provides a relevant model in understanding how PK may relate to paranormal activity. It is useful for investigators to know a bit about his research. Dr. Roll developed the concept of Recurrent Spontaneous PK, or RSPK. This model is interesting and can serve as one possible explanation of hauntings. In lay terms, it is a type of subconscious energy that originates in the mind of a PK agent where objects will move when the agent is at the location (although there are a few exceptions were the agent has been off site). Often, the agent is under some type of stress and subconsciously targets object symbolic of this stress. Events may appear as a type of haunting. Dr. Roll researched numerous PK claims, including the famous Tina Resch case. Resch was a Florida teenager who exhibited profound PK abilities. Media attention surrounded the Resch case, and she was dubbed the "Columbus Poltergeist." Despite being caught faking a few PK incidents, she was also tested in laboratory conditions where she exhibited PK abilities. The documented reality of RSPK is one few contemporary investigators may consider as being one course of "ghostly" activity.

Biology and the Environment

As portals are thought to be related to some sort of geologic or environmental components (such as geomagnetism or frequency synchronization), it is hard to dismiss that the natural world and our own biology may play significant roles in our perception of paranormal events. Some parapsychologists also believe these variables may manifest as paranormal activity.

Many ghost hunters may not like to consider the root of some activity may be very real, scientific elements; some cling to the idea of a tangible spirit that needs assistance. Such sentient creatures may indeed exist, but there are multiple variables present in how paranormal activity is experienced.

Dr. Barry Taff used to work at the University of California Los Angeles's now defunct parapsychology lab. He has conducted over four thousand investigations throughout his vibrant career. Like Auerbach, he believes that an observer is a key variable in hauntings or ghostly activity but in a manner different than what Auerbach hypothesizes. Dr. Taff points out in his book, *Aliens Above, Ghosts Below*, that there seems to be a correlation between the earth's geomagnetism, seizure disorders, and individual ability to become an agent. Dr. Taff is famous for *The Entity* case (the movie that, he points out, was greatly exaggerated). The case featured a single mother named Doris Bither and her four children. Living conditions were horrible in Doris's home, and she had a dysfunctional relationship with her male children. She grew up as an abused child herself and continued this pattern in her battle with alcoholism and abusive relationships.

Doris experienced a variety of phenomena that were also witnessed by others and would be labeled by some as demonic in nature. Her children claimed to see her thrown around her room. Furthermore, she was also being sexually assaulted by something that appeared to be a male entity. Despite the sensationalistic aspects of this case, Dr. Taff believes neurochemical and emotional variables around the client created the activity.

He writes, "This single investigation seemingly appears to reinforce the findings of contemporary academic researchers...that there is some abstract form of relationship between electrochemically unstable individuals and paranormal phenomena." The phenomena moved as Doris relocated from house to house. For Taff, there is a correlation between poltergeist outbreaks (what he feels this was) and temporal lobe activity. What Taff asserts is that the client's emotional state, psychic energy, and instability contributed to a unique situation where she was the agent of activity that externally manifested and witnessed.

His observations are astute. Taff has measured an increase in paranormal activity *and* health issues in areas of high geomagnetism. These physical elements are often hard to adequately assess without specialized equipment most in the ghost hunting community cannot afford and do not know how to use. One can go to the USGS survey and check the seismic and geomagnetic activity of any given location. However, equipment to monitor this during an investigation is far more expensive than most ghost gear and requires some specialized knowledge. It may be difficult for many teams to meaningfully engage in such research, but it remains one important aspect to consider.

Many groups fail to consider how the environment can contribute to spooky or even frightening events. Loyd Auerbach once investigated a home that turned out to be what he coined an "environmental haunting." This house had the classic claims many would consider demonic:

foul smells, headaches and dizziness, balls of fire flying around the house to the extent that they scorched walls, shadow figures, and weird people coming into a barn on the property late at night.

The family made several attempts to get help and was told each time to seek psychological counseling. The owner dismissed his tenants' concerns, so they had few options available to them but to live in a frightening situation. Loyd eventually landed the case after the family complained to a police officer he knew. At first Loyd was skeptical of their claims, but the large number of witnesses piqued his interest. This is a case that many would automatically assume to be malicious, demonic, or negative in nature.

Loyd discovered key environmental factors that when combined, created a seemingly haunted atmosphere. For starters, the house was near a landfill and the foul smells were methane from the nearby decomposing trash. The owner was an architect who built the home with his college students. The material used in construction created a great deal of static electricity which in turn provided the spark for the methane to ignite.

In addition, the house was not level—contributing to the feeling of dizziness. On top of those inconvenient problems, the nearby high-tension power lines created extremely high EMF levels that contributed to the family feeling "off" in the home. (The EMF was so high that their equipment was unable to measure it. It was literally off the charts.) Likewise, one could hear an audible hum from the lines, suggesting that low frequency sounds were one possible factor contributing to hallucinations the tenants experienced. At just the right pitch, low frequency sound can cause eyeball fluid to vibrate. Auerbach wasn't able to measure this variable during this case but offered it as one hypothesis of why the family collectively experienced shadow figures. Additionally, the landlord also forgot to inform the tenants that his students used a loft in the barn at odd hours to study.

No demons were present during Loyd's case but the house was indeed evil (in its own way). Loyd was able to help the tenants get out of their lease due to coding violations. The owner became cooperative at that point. After all, his tenants were literally living in a toxic home.

This particular case is always interesting to me. Not only does it provide excellent "debunking" examples, but it shows what happens when you start to ask noncliched questions about ghosts and hauntings. Nobody took these people seriously. They lived in a frightening, possible dangerous home, and were rescued by paranormal investigators who asked the right questions. Remember, this all started with what was essentially a ghost story and claims from people others thought were just crazy. This case demonstrates how paranormal investigators can do a world of good even in the absence of a ghost (or demon).

Something to Know:

Things as common as cell phone towers, nearby military bases, dumps, and transformers may be variables in paranormal claims. Some investigators live for a ghostly experience at the expense of ruling out some very mundane sources. Be sure to scout out your surroundings at any location you investigate, including going out in the daytime to visually observe the grounds outside the physical building.

PSI Elements

Few are familiar with the role of *psi* (pronounced "sigh") and how it relates to fieldwork and personal paranormal experiences. I have discussed PK/poltergeist cases and the interplay between biology and the environment. Psychokinesis is one element of psi.

Historically, problems arose regarding the use of psychics and mediums. Many mediums were frauds, or at best, highly inconsistent. However, a correlation emerged between what is called psi and what we call ghostly activity. The concept of consciousness is arguably one way in which ESP, telepathy, mediumship, near-death experiences (NDEs), out-of-body experiences (OBEs), and ghostly occurrences materialize. Psi is considered to be "an anomalous processes of information or energy transfer," according to academic researchers Daryl Bem and Charles Honorton. No one is sure how psi works in the mechanical sense, yet serious paranormal investigators are obtaining data that shows something remarkable and unexplainable is occurring. The potential links between psi and the paranormal are therefore intriguing for ghost-hunting teams. We may find there are tangible links between ghostly occurrences and other phenomena like near-death experiences and out-of-body reports.

Traditional survival research involved the living as much as it did the departed: the investigation's focus was mediumship abilities of the living, and psychic impressions were standard protocol. The larger object of study, however, was that of consciousness in the form of survival research. For the first time in investigative history, psi and human consciousness is minimized in favor of detached, technologically based investigation. The role of the observer is now displaced by the role of equipment. The device itself is the medium. There are benefits to this, of course. This type of data is considered to be more objective and scientifically valid. The use of psychics remains highly problematic, considering so many claim to have abilities in the absence of demonstrable proof. The global rise of ghost hunting and the number of teams going into private homes demands a new type of discussion: is it ethical to use psychics who have no proven track record, considering the type of emotional harm that may ensue from unfounded claims?

The role of the human observer (the client, the investigator) may be the most significant aspect of research, as pointed out earlier. If there is an intelligent, disembodied energy present, does it make a sound if no one is present to hear?

Equipment used today primarily measures changes in the physical environment, captures EVP, and documents investigators as they go about their business. While I explore these topics later, we have to admit that there is little evidence that equipment can measure anything beyond that. In an ideal world, we would like to measure *consciousness*, as many theorize it is key in understanding a variety of events, from apparitions to psychical ability to the healing power of prayer and meditation.

....

Something to Know:

Consciousness in this case is not a psychological term (it is more of a subjective one), yet it is becoming a popular subject in fields of scientific and academic inquiry. Some quantum physicists are interested in what role consciousness plays in defining our reality. There are attempts to "map" out how consciousness physically works inside the brain. No one really understands what consciousness is or how to measure it, but it is agreed it does exist at the conceptual level. Researchers often refer to this mystery as "the Problem of Consciousness." The Institute of Noetic Studies (IONS) is one organization that takes a serious look the role of consciousness in NDEs, OBEs, and how "global consciousness" affects our world.

....

I personally enjoy experimenting with technological gadgets. Many investigators, myself included, now count equipment anomalies as a type of personal experience. If a piece of equipment repeatedly responds directly to my questions, for example, that becomes my evidence. I enjoy paranormal events as much as anyone else, but I also understand that it does little to help me understand the mechanisms behind the phenomenon. Data collected on equipment means nothing if there are no hypotheses and philosophical frameworks in place in which to interpret the data.

Psi may also be why some investigators consistently obtain more evidence in general, or find they get more evidence with a particular camera or digital audio recorder. The Experimenter Effect is one example of psi, where investigators subconsciously project thoughts on to the equipment. Investigators may not find this explanation as glamorous as a ghost, but it shores up intriguing proof regarding the mind's potential, also providing data that psi can influence the environment.

The psi role also looks at esoteric investigative methods, like magick and occult aspects, as these two essentially deal with "mind over matter" in their own capacity. Rather than paint it black as many people do, I believe this is another manifestation of psi. In this equation, someone who enters investigation with intent to contact a certain type of energy will probably be able to do just that.

Psi components are in place by way of investigator intent and manifestation in the physical environment as equipment interaction (EVP included), rapping, or personal experience. These phenomena can emerge from disembodied intelligence or be subconscious projections of those present in body.

No real consensus exists regarding how psi works—or even what creates a ghost or haunting. Yet the idea of psi is viable among academic-based researchers. Consciousness models do not exclude the possibility that Aunt Norah's soul is just checking in on loved ones. It actually offers a conceptual and philosophical framework for that to occur.

Psi provides the most viable scientific and metaphysical model to understand these events, and it is one serious investigators need to consider.

Quantum Theory, Consciousness, and Ghosts

Having just discussed consciousness, let's discuss the quantum. There are many, many other tangents one can go off on but as this book intends to be accessible and reader-friendly, I'll try to keep it simple!

Quantum psychics are becoming the new go-to accessory for paranormal enthusiasts. As mentioned earlier, the concept of quantum consciousness offers theoretical ways to discuss out-of-body and near-death experiences, providing great fodder for those interested in the role consciousness may play in paranormal activity. These topics are fascinating and may shore up links to our understanding of ghosts. It may be limiting in scope to study ghostly events as a phenomenon separate from other components of the mind, but it is the current reality of the ghost-hunting scene.

Ghosts, spirits, specters—whatever you wish to call them—are fascinating in their own right. But like all great characters, they have a backstory. Their particular backstory may involve strings, entanglement, wormholes, and zero point gravity fields.

Quantum theory postulates many things, but the aspects I want to highlight consider the links between consciousness, our ability to access other "realms," and what role a few concepts may play. Let me state that I am not a physicist or even close to being one. I also want to preface that this discussion is merely philosophical in nature. These ideas may have some scientific resonance relating to ghosts and hauntings, but they remain ethereal ones to test out in the field.

We understand and accept that energy cannot be destroyed and that it only changes form. That is a truism today, but there was a time when even that concept seemed out there.

One aspect of quantum physics expands upon the nature of energy, matter, and reality's underpinnings. One particular idea is nonlocality, which is when "two particles of a complementary pair can be separated by vast spatial distances, yet still remain instantaneous communication with one another" as explained by Marie D. Jones. It appears that this information is transferred even faster than the speed of light. According to Newtonian physics, these things aren't supposed to happen. What it suggests is that some sort of entanglement—or "psychic" connection—between particles underlines the basis of all existing processes in our world. This explanation is a gross oversimplification, of course, but Albert Einstein aptly dubbed this as "spooky action at a distance."

Another element to know is that certain particles react differently depending on the observer. This behavior suggests that observer intent can influence the minute, underlying variables of reality. There is a very real connection between matter and the mind. Consciousness studies advocates assert that our attitude about life can actually impact our living reality and there seems to be some scientific evidence to back this up!

Quantum particles are so small and infinite that their qualities average out at the everyday, observable scale. Yet these theories do offer profound insights to how consciousness may work and how ghosts emerge in our dimensional space. For some, ghosts may be interdimensional travelers able to "bleed through" membranes and appear as a holograph in our dimension. For others, our consciousness is the quantum traveler able to bring forth an apparitional sighting from some other undefined, uncharted space.

What role does zero point energy (ZPE) play in this, and what exactly is it? ZPE is the lowest level (ground state) of quantum energy present in all things, even at absolute zero temperatures or in a vacuum. It persists throughout the entire universe. It is the invisible "force field" that holds everything together.

Chris Schlosser of TAPS Academy and the Virginia Paranormal Society and I were emailing about these ideas, as we were both reading on these topics at the same time. He messaged me saying he had a headache from it all. I messaged him back and agreed, pointing out that while I like this philosophy, I was unsure how to apply it to actual investigation.

Chris is a forensic toxicologist by training, so he is a smart guy. The next morning, I guess he nursed his headache to come up with a great way quantum consciousness, zero point theory, and ghosts may align, so to speak. I'll let Chris explain it in his own words, lest I get a headache trying to do it myself:

Question: How Does Consciousness Survive Death?
Chris: Hmm ... we are always concerned about what happens to consciousness after death, but the answer may be in how consciousness is created in the first place.

Chris explains:

So, one of the big questions regarding the existence of ghosts is really how our consciousness survives death. When people approach the other end of this, we typically ask, "How does consciousness or the spirit enter the body?"

What if that is the wrong question to ask? I think we are approaching this the wrong way. What if the body precedes the spirit? What if our brain essentially "assembles" our conscious-self at a quantum level starting from the functioning of our brain waves during fetal development?

Research in consciousness and psi ability seems to suggest that our brain is somehow pulling information from a universal source (i.e., the zero point field) at the quantum level. What if the brain also assembles our consciousness and spirit at the quantum level? Basically this is taking this universal energy and arranging into an organized system within our body.

A real working correlation is how the human body uses food as energy and creates more organized information rich molecules such as DNA and RNA. This follows the second law of thermodynamics. We create a more organized system and increase the disorder of our surroundings. The human body is one of the few systems that lowers entropy because our body is a closed system. We essentially create a more organized system from the less ordered surroundings that allows us the chemical energy to keep our bodies running. Our physical bodies can survive for a relatively long period of time without taking in new energy sources.

Therefore, let us hypothesize that we create our consciousness at a quantum level by creating order out of a universal energy, and what we create persists for a time after death. This, or course, would vary depending on the individual and the amount of energy present. In addition, if consciousness survives, it would possibly be able to interact with natural sources of energy to maintain or slow its dissociation and extend its life after the death of the body.

However, as holds true with chemical energy, entropy and disorder are always increasing, therefore the consciousness will inevitably no longer be able to sustain itself without the body and simply dissociates back into the universal energy field (i.e., the zero point field).

What this offers is one potential explanation combining consciousness studies, biology, metaphysics, and ghostly occurrences. Now, back to our regularly scheduled programming...

....

Something to Know:

I've just thrown out a great deal of information so I feel a basic summary is useful. The popular definition of a ghost is the remaining disembodied soul or consciousness of the departed. As you have read, however, there are several competing theories on what causes things to go bump in the night, including the idea that the living and the natural environment may be a type of generator or amplifier for spirit activity. There are books written by other authors on these individual topics alone. I cannot suggest that one hypothesis is better than another, but I can recommend that it is important to know the basic research overview. These things do affect what one does on investigation.

....

Before we get into the real nitty-gritty of ghost hunting, it is important to know just how the concept of ghosts (and their study) has changed throughout history.

2: History of Ghosts and Their Hunters

Earlier, I provided an overview of contemporary concepts around ghosts and hauntings. In the previous chapter, I highlighted a few investigators such as Loyd Auerbach, Troy Taylor, Hans Holzer, and Joshua Warren. However, there is a long history and a large number of other personalities who have shaped what you and I do in investigation.

Tales of the supernatural are as old as humanity. There is nothing new in the "ghost story," but what has changed is the way we understand and speculate on spectral matters. The earliest stories were orally transmitted, often morphing into new stories as they were passed along. Today, story travels faster than ever. Media technology such as the Internet and digital video, audio, and photography, define paranormal sightings, including sightings of UFO and Bigfoot, on a global basis at instantaneous speed. Some ghost hunting groups even stream investigations live!

Many paranormal teams feel they are being innovative and original in their approaches, and sometimes investigators do exhibit interesting creativity. But it is rare that we actually do anything new in terms of philosophy. Ghost hunting has been around for a while. Unlike the breakneck speed of the Internet or the nicely edited TV shows we watch, real research is an incredible slow process that was sticky-taped to 150 years of parapsychology's field and lab work.

Physical researchers (and later, parapsychologists) investigated hauntings long before paranormal reality TV entered the scene. At one time, parapsychology was a recognized academic field, and there were programs at Duke University, Princeton, and John F. Kennedy University, among others. University of California Los Angeles (UCLA) had a parapsychology lab. These days, one has to go to the United Kingdom to get a credible, accredited academic degree in the field.

Parapsychology is concerned with the role of psi. The field studies phenomena like ESP, near-death experiences (NDEs), and general psychical ability underline the conceptual model of psi. Ghosts and hauntings were never at the core of parapsychological study although survival research was the initial instigator into the study of larger phenomena.

However, a few academically trained parapsychologists still operate and those who do are a bit disgruntled over the contemporary amateur ghost hunting scene. Many are critical of how many ghost hunters have entered the field since the advent of paranormal reality TV—people who often know very little of ghost hunting's history and academic legacy. Being an amateur astronomer or bird watcher carries a positive connotation, for example. These amateur hobbyists are part of a movement called citizen science where lay people contribute to larger public discussions by documenting celestial or bird phenomena (the latter of which helps policy makers monitor species and environmental change, for example.) Yet to be an amateur ghost hunter carries a negative connotation in more academic communities not because of the subject matter itself, but because so many paranormalists do not follow any sound methodology whatsoever. On top of that, the language and way ghost hunters talk about their avocation can make some scientists literally cringe.

Everyone acknowledges that the appearance of some wonderful investigators on TV unlocked the doors to mass appeal. It is also easier than ever to do research and receive cases. After all, Americans love to talk about their experiences, and many sites desire to be haunted. A decade ago, a haunted label may have been a liability. Unfortunately, parapsychologists and many cast members have noticed a *decrease* in historical and philosophy knowledge among newcomers concerning ghosts, hauntings, and related subjects. There are pockets of technical and investigative innovation, yet many components are lacking. Some observers feel that the popularity of paranormal investigation will not help the field advance unless there are some dramatic improvements in the following areas: appreciation for the legacy of psychical research, attention to ethics and legal issues potentially facing investigators, and better documenting of investigation and data.

The Unseen Element

It is important to understand the cultural and philosophical context behind ghostly concepts. First, reports of haunting-like events have occurred throughout history. Some early accounts were later discovered to have a sound scientific explanation (like eclipses, for example, which were once thought to be a sign from the gods). The first documented ghost hunt is thought to be in 100 AD, recorded by Pliny the Younger. The Bible speaks of spirits, and all holy texts address the existence of unseen beings in some form or another. In some cases, these beings or angels or demons. In other cases, as with Islam's Qur'an, they are interdimensional inhabitants with free will (the djinn). Pagans and other religious traditions express a belief in earth spirits and other sentient energies.

All these concepts are as old as civilization. They are also all related to contemporary ideas about ghosts and hauntings in one way or another.

The Bible offers a cosmology many use to interpret paranormal events. Good, evil, angels, and demons are all there. The Qu'ran nods to different dimensions. Quantum physicists now theorize that there are at least twelve dimensions—others say there are infinite number and that we live in a multiverse rather than universe. These dimensions are occurring simultaneously. One hypothesis is that some paranormal events are interdimensional bleed-through. This is one possible explanation for alien and Bigfoot sightings, as well as for ghosts.

How do consciousness, energy, and human experience link up? The Tibetan Book of the Dead speaks of how meditating monks can manifest *tul-pas*, or beings created from thought. This idea relates back psi or consciousness studies. Psychical researchers believe that psi is a key component to ghosts, as discussed earlier. However, if you really want to be a serious ghost hunter, it is important to understand how the history of ideas frames certain parts of the discussion.

Shamanism

Humanity's earliest religions were defined by communicating with the unseen. The shaman was the messenger between the living and the spirit world. Shamanic practice varied among cultures—and still does—but all involves a living agent communicating with the spirit world, having basic healing abilities, and generally being able to delve into the unseen. This was the earliest form of mediumship and psychical ability, and may arguable be the foundation for today's monotheistic belief systems. It harks back to humanity's need to search for something bigger than us and understand the world as a spiritual experience in addition to a physical one.

The foundation of shamanism was animism, the belief in a type of life force embodied in both living and nonliving creations. It is the assumption that a type of life force (or energy) exists in all things. Animism is almost like a catch phrase for "energy," a concept that remains with us today.

Christian Cosmology

Christianity has influenced the way most Western societies deal with ghosts, although many long held ideas predate formal religion. There is no single Christian cosmology, of course, but the basic elements involve a belief in heaven, hell, and purgatory (for Catholics). The official policy of most religious institutions is that ghosts do not exist, save the Holy Ghost.

One minority view held by some Christians is that all paranormal activity is caused by demons trying to trick humanity in some way. This extreme view (though it is not popular), is one that asserts humanity to be in a type of spiritual warfare between good and evil.

Most Christians who believe in ghosts also accept demons but do not believe demons are behind all activity. Some may feel that ghosts are departed souls unable to move on due to fear, unfinished business, or a desire to stay behind and be close to loved ones. As one person suggested, free will extends to the afterlife, so ghosts can decide to stay or to go.

Other Christian-based thought posits that ghosts are trapped souls, most likely those belonging in purgatorial state, sometimes needing prayer or intervention from the living in order to move on. In this context, some believe it is not "natural" for ghosts to remain in this realm although it does not mean they are evil.

Occult Perspective

The esoteric or occult perspective played a larger public role in paranormal investigation until paranormal reality TV redefined the discussion. Pagans, Wiccans, and occultists still actively participate in investigation. (Note that Pagans are not necessarily occultists and vice versa.)

A misnomer surrounds the word "occult." To many, it denotes something sinister, dark, or Satanic. There may be individuals who seek the dark arts, yet most occultists are not evil in nature. They work within a particular philosophical framework that, like parapsychology, has a historical context. This perspective really delves into hidden knowledge, or information that is beyond being measured. In a way, the "scientific" definition has co-opted what is an intrinsic occult nature of research. Surely, today's contemporary investigation is often technically valid and derived from seemingly objective approaches. However, occultist history has influenced science, religion, Spiritualism, and ghost jaunts more than most admit.

One idea (similar to what Hindus believe about the afterlife) suggests the world is composed of different astral bodies. The physical body is but one manifestation. There are different subtle levels, and ghosts exist (according to some) in the etheric and astral. Author Konstantinos, a well-known occultist and EVP researcher, suggests that spirits exist on different levels. Famed Wiccan Raymond Buckland also accepts this view. The souls on the lower realm or often not as "evolved" or even as kind as souls are in the higher realm, but it is easier for lower-realm souls to communicate with us. The astral elements may be accessed through different vibrational qualities. The term "resonance" is also being used in other circles to describe this concept, which has root in quantum physics.

This philosophical framework is shared by some Spiritualists and even Christian investigators, thus being more influential than we realize. Finally, emerging aspects of quantum physics and the idea of a holographic universe allows scientific to conceive of parallel dimensions that may on occasion bleed through due to resonance. This is all speculative when it comes to ghosts but is worthy of discussion.

Society and Culture

It is noted that reports of ghostly phenomena increase during times of social and cultural change. What does this mean? Does psychic ability somehow spike during times of mass unrest and instability? Or is it socially constructed, meaning that it changes context throughout history? There is a connection between science, society, technology, and ghostly claims. For example, many teams in the United States have noticed an increase in cases with military families. There is no doubt that such families are undergoing tremendous, unique stresses. Do these conditions attract ghosts or is this an external manifestation of personal stress? Whatever the root cause, societies find special meaning in ghost stories that help them deal with newly emerging issues of the day.

Another example of this is the lack of contemporary cases involving dopplegängers (a "twin") or crisis apparitions, which are sightings of the living by others at the time of death or during stressful moments. A hundred and twenty years ago, there were more case reports of this phenomenon than there were of ghosts!

Finally, we cannot overlook the impact of paranormal media and how it has made it cool to be haunted. This means that teams get more cases but it also means that is may sometimes be harder to really explore what phenomena is taking place. American now enjoys a fairly accessible "ghostly" culture.

Who's Who Among Ghost Hunters

So far, we have reviewed some basic hypothesis behind ghosts. Some of these overlap and some contradict each other completely. But just as important as the ideas are the people and institutions behind the ideas.

We reviewed some contemporary thinkers on ghosts and hauntings in the previous chapter. Let us look at other personalities and institutions that have shaped today's paranormal investigative scene.

Catholic Church

Don't laugh—the Church is probably the most influential force in how ghosts and hauntings are culturally understood in Western societies. Also, Catholic priests and bishops were some of the earliest investigators as they attempted to document strangeness. Of course, these events were often interpreted in the realm of good and evil (angels and demons). Likewise, some early Christian thinkers were also students of the occult, so there is some overlap in ideas of the unseen world. These convergent influences remain with us today. What did the Catholic Church contribute? Purgatory, a religious framework for understanding ghosts, and early documentation of haunted locations and poltergeist activity.

Spiritualism

Spiritualism is a philosophical and religious movement that emerged in America during the mid-1800s after two sisters in upstate New York claimed to communicate with a spirit in their home through a series of rappings. Spirit communication was not a new idea and was already occurring in America and Europe. What distinguished the American emergence was how quickly the concept became part of public culture, thus introducing the masses to the world's first "paracelebrities."

Some of the most popular inaugural figures of the Spiritualism movement were the Fox Sisters. They became famous and ushered in an age of public interest in communicating with the dead. Spiritualism accepts that life continues after death and spirits have the ability to reach back to the living and vice versa. Most Spiritualists do believe in the Christian God and accept that spirit communication does not contradict Biblical teachings. What is particularly noteworthy about Spiritualism is how it popularized séances and mediumship, but the fraudulent nature of some mediums encouraged debunking and organized scientific inquiry into psychical ability. Which leads us to ...

Ghost Club of London

Founded in 1862, this was the first known group to gather in the name of ghosts and psychical research. Spiritualism was now a growing global phenomenon and many wanted to research the claims. Sir William Crookes was a member, as well as Charles Dickens, although I cannot say that this influenced the latter's Ghosts of Christmas Past, Present, and Future.

Founders of the Society for Psychical Research (SPR) and the American Society for Psychical Research (ASPR)

The SPR formed on the heels of the Ghost Club. One important note is that many figures were women. A year later, the ASPR was founded and is still kicking today (in fact, so are the Ghost Club and the SPR). What did the SPR contribute? Systematic documentation of experimentation of hauntings, reports, and eyewitness accounts, as well as a community of like-minded individuals. They also published some of earliest cogent literature on reports in the 1886 *Phantasm of the Living* (in which most reports turned out not to be ghosts but apparitions of the living!).

William James

Sometimes overlooked by the ghost-hunting crowd, the father of psychology was a supporter of psychical research, and he sometimes endured personal and professional ridicule. He was an early advocate—maybe the most vocal—to suggest applying the scientific method to paranormal research. He was a founding member of both the SPR and ASPR. James was eloquent in how he connected psychical research with the emerging field of academic sciences and the quest for spiritual belief. In a way, James characterizes how many people today view the paranormal: at a crossroads between personal faith, scientific explanation, and ridicule. He was an intellectual thinker with faith in science and the metaphysical nature of unexplained events. A few of us have coined a phrase when facing larger questions concerning the paranormal: WWJD? Most people assume it means "What Would Jason (Hawes) Do?" Nope, we ask, "What Would James Do?"

Harry Price

He coined the term "ghost hunter" with his book in 1938. This independently wealthy magician and researcher popularized the use of equipment. He also actively engaged media, and like his contemporary paranormal TV cast members, suffered strong criticism for it. He really formulated the first how-to manual, along with case studies. Many cite him as the Father of Ghost Hunting, but that is erroneous. His contribution is that he merely popularized the term by using the media and helped introduce equipment and accessible methodology to the field.

J. B. Rhine

J. B. Rhine ran the university-based Duke Parapsychology Lab from 1927 to 1965. He was the first person to apply laboratory methods to the study of psi, concentrating on ESP. Dr. Rhine was motivated by his desire for proof of the soul's survival. He realized that one could not put a ghost in a lab. However, one could study people who felt they communicated with ghosts. Dr. Rhine revolutionized parapsychology and provided institutional support for research into hauntings and psychokinesis. Today, this work continues at the Rhine Research Center (RRC)in Durham. A small part of The RRC's interest involves hauntings while most research revolves around the larger concept of psi and consciousness.

Early Well-Known Investigators

There are some well-known personalities who are prolific and have been around for decades helping to define the public face of the paranormal. The following are individuals I've identified as major players. This is my personal list and any omissions on my part should be promptly forgiven.

Ed and Lorraine Warren

Known for their investigations around more negative cases, they were made famous by Amityville Case and other high-profile hauntings. They founded the New England Society for Psychic Research (NESPR) in 1952. They have been integral part of the community and have greatly influenced the Paranormal Research Society's culture (Ryan Buell and *Paranormal State*). Ed and Lorraine worked with many in the community and are dearly loved by their supporters. Ed passed away in 2006 but Lorraine still makes public appearances.

John Zaffis

Nephew of Ed and Lorraine, he learned from them and became an investigator known for focusing on demonology. He also researched various types of phenomena, including haunted objects. The author of several books on demons, he has made appearances on several TV shows and documentaries, and authored several books detailing his long career. His Museum of the Paranormal showcases haunted objects from around the world. This fascination and his longstanding participation in the community led him to SyFy's *Haunted Collector* in the summer of 2011. He was an early mentor to Jason Hawes and TAPS. Zaffis, along with the Warrens, is influential in popularizing "demonology" although he investigates different many different types of cases.

Rosemary Ellen Guiley

There are many contemporary female investigators, but she is one of the most prolific authors to produce paranormal related matter. Her research is vast. She is able to link up various paranormal concepts to a wide range of ideas. Some suggest that her approach is more New Age than scientific. Rosemary has seen and heard almost everything possible and remains one of the most cogent resources on any paranormal related research, from faeries to hauntings.

Internet Stars

The Internet forever changed paranormal investigation and served as a precursor to today's paranormal community. There are a few individuals who first took to the Internet, and their presence changed the very types of discussions people had about ghosts and evidence. The Internet itself is a personality in the community, but so are those who pioneered group culture online.

Dave Oester

Dave Oester and his wife Sharon founded the International Ghost Hunters Society, the first online network for paranormal enthusiasts. The highly controversial orb theory is attributed to him, a theory that Jason Hawes of TAPS sharply criticized online in the 1990s. However, Oester was the first person to establish an online community of paranormal enthusiasts and set an early standard for wide online engagement. He still believes that some orbs (not all) are related to paranormal activity and proudly claims to be the "Orb Theory father."

Richard Senate

Along with Oester, Richard Senate was one of the very first paranormal investigators to establish an online presence in the early 1990s. He was a prolific writer on haunted stories, and was a contributor to Ghostvillage.com until 2007. He feels that his contribution to the field is the idea of a "trigger object" being used in investigation. Mr. Senate was seen as a guest on Travel Channel's *Paranormal Challenge* in 2010, thus perhaps marking a comeback into the larger paranormal public.

The Atlantic Paranormal Society (TAPS)

Not long after Oester and Senate established an online presence, TAPS founded their first site. It was distinctive in that it avoided overuse of clichéd images. They become well know after publicly debating Oester's orb theory with an online article. Jason Hawes and Grant Wilson were a bit younger than many others in the community and particularly tech savvy and different in their approach. Soon, their site was getting hits from all over the world. This eventually led to consulting on TV shows like MTV's *Fear*. In 2002, a *New York Times* article profiled them on a case. The next day, producers started calling for a show, and this ultimately lead to *Ghost Hunters* on SyFy in 2004. (American production companies were already seeking to duplicate the success of *Most Haunted* in the United Kingdom). The rest, as they say in show business, is history. *Ghost*

Hunters and TAPS have greatly influenced investigative culture and public understanding of ghosts. None of it, however, would have been possible without that TAPS site.

Ghostvillage.com

Started by Jeff Belanger in 1999, this is a large resource for anything ghost related, from research to popular culture. If you search, you will find everything there, from interviews with people on this list to discussions about technology. Thousands of people from all over the world have paranormal encounters published at the site. Ghostvillage.com is a hub for all information and had a huge impact on how people understand the paranormal. Jeff went on to be a best-selling paranormal author and has no doubt influenced paranormal investigators. It is also feasible to suggest that many paranormal reality TV shows have delved into Ghostvillage.com's vaults for locations and stories. For Belanger, he believes in the power of the "story," for ghost stories start—and often end—as just that: the story.

Paranormal Research Society (PRS)

The PRS-initiated Uni-Con was founded at Penn State, and was the largest paranormal themed conference at the time. The Univ-Con and PRS's existence eventually led to A & E's *Paranormal State*, which ran from 2007 to 2011. The PRS is interesting in that it is academically minded with reference to parapsychology, yet the organization also acknowledges and incorporates spiritual and metaphysical components in their research. The PRS remains active, with a membership body. On occasion, they hold online classes and sponsor field trips at haunted sites for the public to attend, which include lectures and investigation. The PRS is distinguished by its diverse demographic as well as being able to attract an academically oriented group.

3: Paranormal Investigation— The Good, The Bad, and The Weird

Different Approaches

The whole concept of "ghost hunting" has changed dramatically since paranormal reality TV emerged. In the past, psychical researchers and parapsychologists studied apparitional and psychic phenomena related to hauntings. These investigators had intellectual pedigrees, and in more contemporary times, were university trained. Their study was not limited to just ghosts and focused on other issues like extrasensory perception, telekinesis, mediumship, and psychokinesis (PK). It was a package-deal sort of thing.

The original ghost hunters were steeped in the tradition of physical research, something contemporary ghost hunters displace. For the first time in investigative history, the role of the medium and human agent are displaced in order to privilege technical equipment. In today's reality, the equipment has become the medium itself.

There are positive and negative aspects to these developments. In the past, it was a bit uncommon to come across a parapsychologist or paranormal researcher. Alternatively, there may have been one quietly living in your neighborhood. Social stigma surrounded these topics until about a decade ago. Today, being a ghost hunter is a "neat" thing to do. There are investigation teams in almost every American city. Some say there are too many people now investigating with too little merit behind the efforts.

Amateur ghost hunting (as well as ufology and Bigfoot searches) emerged in conjunction with handheld technology. As video and audio technology shrank in size and costs, more people were able to use devices for this type of research. The Internet, likewise, created communities of enthusiasts who were able to interact with one another in unprecedented ways. These elements were precursors to reality TV as well as how we currently organize our investigations.

All of these variables determine paranormal investigation to be a group-based endeavor. Joining a team is similar to the bowling leagues of America's past; it provides socializing, a sense of belonging, and a call to adventure. Often, ghost hunting encourages intellectual stimulation and some old-fashioned spiritual soul-searching. It is a way to get a very personal look at history and phenomenal experiences.

Let us talk about the investigative scene, for it is a world of its own. I do not hide that I came into the "field" because of paranormal reality TV. I suspect that many reading this book can say the same. But I certainly pay homage to what came before.

The game has changed, however. The community used to be small and everybody knew everybody else. People differed in philosophy and approach, but there is now overbearing competition for media attention, and "staking a territory" exists where it didn't before. Today there are various breeds of investigators. If you like to go out and have a good time, you are a legend tripper. Some want to help the living and the dead. Great! Some people just want to be on TV, while others just want to do real research.

I have identified four dominant contemporary approaches to paranormal investigation—others may be able to think of more and group them differently. There are many teams who overlap several approaches, but these four main categories sum up what most teams are doing.

Adventure-Based Investigator

Some investigators just want to have fun. They desire to explore personal interests and ghost stories. They are what I call adventure-based investigators, or actual ghost hunters. Theirs is often an enjoyable, social way to learn about local folklore and explore the unknown. Adventure-based investigation (or legend tripping, as author Jeff Belanger calls it), is a harmless, educational way to have fun as long as people are ethical and responsible. This means no trespassing, and ideally, not going into homes of distressed individuals. Ghost hunters may organize around meetup or Facebook groups and often do large group investigations. Some may eventually form a smaller group of like-minded folks. A few will morph into serious researchers. Adventurers are often generally interested in paranormal experiences but may not always have the patience required for the real nitty-gritty of investigation (like hours of evidence review and historical research). Some groups, like AdventureMyths, love the investigative thrill that comes from historical sites and also do a great deal of background research and engage in careful evidence analyses. Their goal is to produce short documentaries of the investigation that they hand back to the sites.

Client-Based Investigators

Some investigators desire to help clients who feel that they have paranormal issues in their homes or businesses. The Atlantic Paranormal Society (TAPS) has operated on this philosophy from the early 1990s and has popularized this particular motivation. They are client-based investigators. To be realistic, investigators cannot always find evidence of the paranormal, but client-based teams can certainly find alternative explanations or provide support. The primary objective of such groups is to help a client feel better, because sometimes the answers just aren't there. This is a very important distinction to make, because groups working with the wrong motivations can do great emotional harm to clients. Within this category are teams that take a spiritual and religious approach. Others take a purely debunking perspective, and most are probably a mixture of both.

Spiritual-Based Investigators

Spiritual-based investigators often work off of some type of spiritual or religious principle, be it Christian, Pagan, or merely metaphysically based. In some cases, such investigators who work with living clients are also concerned with spirit rescue, or helping the departed cross over. In other cases, some deal with negative hauntings or possession cases. There are certain historical, religious, and philosophical perspectives that inform this approach. One thing that distinguishes this particular type of investigator is that many feel literally called to do such work. The Paranormal Research Society (PRS), made famous by *Paranormal State*, personifies this perspective for many. They are concerned with the well-being of the living and the dead.

Research-Based Investigators

Others are invested in research-based investigation, meaning that they prefer cases that do not involve distressed clients. These teams often focus on historic or public properties, or locations where a client is curious rather than afraid. Teams who prioritize this perspective are looking for scientific explanations, or even to completely debunk paranormal claims when possible. The goal is to obtain credible evidence that can augment scientific discussion on the matter. These groups have room to be experimental and use prototype equipment. Research-based investigators may deal with private, client cases but are sometimes a bit removed from the more spiritual-based philosophies.

Role of Psychics

All perspectives may use psychics or mediums on investigation in differing capacities. There seems to be higher value placed on psychics among those who are spiritual-based. However, there are actual scientific ways to incorporate psychic ability on investigation.

In truth, many groups have a little of all the above perspectives. With this in mind, it is important to know not only what you believe, but also what motivates you to become an investigator.

Regardless of why someone is ghost hunting, the avocation is honorable and fun. To do it ethically and responsibly takes some common sense. Maybe you are interested in the type of investigation that may one day help advance the field—that takes some hard work and patience!

What Do You Believe?

It is increasingly important for investigators to understand their own personal beliefs and how it may affect their own ghost hunting.

I have developed several online surveys for the paranormal community. These are helpful in helping you determine what type of investigation may be most intellectually satisfying for you and what you really believe about ghosts.

So I recommend you get a pen or pencil and take this little self-assessment—just for fun! There are no right or wrong answers.

What Do You Believe—A Self-Assessment

(Check all answers that apply to you).

What Are Ghosts?

❑ Ghosts are souls of the departed that occupy our realm

❑ Ghosts are souls of the departed that live on the other side of the veil, and can cross over to our side

- ❑ Ghosts are energy forms
- ❑ Ghosts are leftover aspects or our personalities
- ❑ Ghosts are something we create, like thought forms
- ❑ Ghosts are some type of unexplained process at the quantum level
- ❑ Ghosts are demons or other types of nonhumans
- ❑ Ghosts can be all of the above
- ❑ I am not sure what a ghost is
- ❑ I do not believe in ghosts

Which statements represent your personal beliefs about what happens when we die?

- ❑ We immediately go to Heaven or Hell
- ❑ We go to Purgatory
- ❑ We are reincarnated
- ❑ We go into a type of suspended soul sleep until Jesus returns
- ❑ We go into a type of suspended soul sleep until Judgment Day (not necessarily from a Christian perspective)
- ❑ We merely change into a different type of energy
- ❑ We remain in this realm for a while until we are ready to move on
- ❑ We go to the next spiritual plane
- ❑ We just die and that is it
- ❑ We go to Heaven, Hell, or whatever place we believe in
- ❑ I do not know what happens after we die

What is your motivation for doing paranormal investigation?

- ❑ I want to learn about paranormal theory and history of investigation
- ❑ I want to learn creative and artistic ways to document the investigation
- ❑ I want to experiment with cool equipment
- ❑ I want to conduct various experiments
- ❑ I want to help homeowners
- ❑ I am interested in demonology and spiritual warfare
- ❑ I am interested in learning how the world works
- ❑ I want to develop my own intuitive abilities
- ❑ I am interested in having paranormal experiences
- ❑ I am interested in being someone valued for my ideas and contributions

In your opinion, what causes a ghost?

- ❑ They have unfinished businesses
- ❑ They are afraid or unable to cross over
- ❑ They want to stay behind and check on loved ones
- ❑ They can come and go whenever they want
- ❑ They can come and go at specific times for specific reasons
- ❑ A living agent as a form of psychokinesis may generate a "ghost"
- ❑ A "ghost" is merely a scientific yet unexplained natural process we do not yet understand
- ❑ I have no idea

Which statements reflect how you feel the "other side" works?

- ❏ There are certain rules that ghosts/spirits must follow
- ❏ Purgatory is the "other side"
- ❏ We are merely experiencing a holographic aspect of the multiverse
- ❏ There are many dimensions occupied by various life forms/energies
- ❏ Ghosts are merely unidentified energies and we are experiencing natural—not supernatural—phenomena
- ❏ Ghosts can see us all the time but we can't see them unless they want us to
- ❏ Certain conditions have to be just right in order for us to communicate across the veil
- ❏ The "other side" is something accessible to us at any given time through the use of our consciousness

———————————

Now that you have taken this self-assessment, really think about what you believe and how you feel about ghosts, hauntings, the afterlife, the role of religion, and science. Hopefully you now have a better sense of what you believe and what you may want to accomplish in investigation. Maybe write out your own personal statement and put it away somewhere. Revisit that statement in a few months, or even a year, and see if your ideas have changed. This type of journey is often transformative; many people find their beliefs undergo dramatic change, and there is nothing wrong with that.

The Community and the Field

For many, paranormal investigation is the start of a great journey that helps individuals grow intellectually, spiritually, and creatively. You may already be on that journey, or you may have discovered from the self-assessment that you really do not yet know what you want to get from being a paranormal investigator. Maybe you just feel it is something you need to do.

Before we get too involved in this discussion, it is necessary to clearly define some commonly used terms in the paranormal community. In fact, let's distinguish the *community* from the *field*.

For the sake of this book, I define the paranormal community as a collection of individuals, investigators, and reality TV show fans who openly express interest and invest in the newly emerged paranormal pop culture. This includes those who attend paranormal-themed conferences, participate in the vibrant online paranormal Internet community, group ghost hunts, and perhaps have membership in a hardcore group. The community is the paranormal public face. Most of us start in the community by hobnobbing with our favorite personality at a conference or trying to hang with a local team.

The field, however, is quiet and constitutes a smaller component of the community. This is where actual investigation and research takes place. The field has less emphasis on the entertainment and media aspects and more focus on investigating and philosophy. Many involved in the field are also part of the community, but not all in the community are involved in the field. There is a distinction, and often very different types of conversations take place in the field. It is the kind of thing that many paranormal reality TV fans may not find interesting or entertaining. In a way, you almost have to earn your way in through doing good work, demonstrating professionalism, and networking. But those who are really interested in research and investigation will eventually gravitate this way.

Perhaps the biggest influence of TV is the emphasize on what I call the "Black T-Shirt syndrome," meaning the rush to go out and form teams based on T-shirt design and logo. (Some see this more as a social activity than a research one.) Now, I'm not making fun of teams who wear black T-shirts. I like black and own a few team shirts myself. But the point is group culture now defines how we access the paranormal in terms of investigation—and it is far more work than most realize.

Group Work

Ghost hunting teams and groups now exist everywhere. There are ghost hunters in Afghanistan, Israel, and probably even Timbuktu. For sure, this interest is now a solid part of mainstream American society, regardless of what show is in vogue, and will remain popular for a long time into the future. Ghost hunting is social activity just as much as it can be a research-oriented one.

There are many great books and online resources providing advice on how to start your own group. Still, many people have no idea how to go about it. This is often due to not knowing enough like-minded people in your area, or a lack of awareness regarding what resources are needed.

I will explain the process of getting a group off the ground, and let me make something clear: it is a ton of work. There are plenty of less labor-intensive ways to get a ghost fix, if that is what you want. Some people feel absolutely compelled to investigate for a variety of reasons. If this is something in which you are willing to invest time, energy, and money, then get ready!

I've talked to several investigators around the world. Most suggest to ask yourself first what you are trying to discover. Do you just want to see a ghost or have a personal experience? If so, that's just a matter of wandering around haunted locations. Legend tripping is just that—it doesn't take more than a little bit of responsibility and scouting accessible haunted locations.

Many people are interested in the real deal. A collective response from the investigators I spoke with is summed up in the following statement: If you want to research, then identify what you want to capture and do research on that particular field. For example, if you want to study EVP or disembodied voices, do research on that equipment. Many groups do not use the equipment properly, something I discuss later in the book. The collective voice also agrees on the need to do research on the history of whatever one is studying—and there is a body of literature from psychical research, parapsychology, and even EVP work.

I have personally noticed that a lot of groups—especially spawning from the television series—see these things on TV and go out and capture evidence they don't understand. There are plenty of people wanting to do exactly what they see on TV—nothing less and nothing more, and that is OK if individuals are able to present that as their motivation.

If one is really sincere about scientific investigation, reading the literature is far more important than buying black T-shirts from your group or the coolest new EMF meter. Some groups are motivated by a strong desire to help clients. This is a noble endeavor, but also very slippery terrain. One has to be very focused, ethical, and aware of a variety of legal issues before you enter someone's home.

The collective brings up a good point—the first step is to identify what you want to do. Ask yourself some questions: Is your desire to just have an experience, assist homeowners, help spirits cross over, or do research? The first step is to explore and be honest about your motivations. Understanding what you want to accomplish will help you get the most out of whatever path you choose. Be aware of your beliefs about ghosts and hauntings because it will influence how you investigate and probably whom you investigate with, as well.

The second step is to meet others with similar interests. I am surrounded by so many ghost-hunting friends that I take it for granted many do no have access to a paranormal-friendly community.

How to Meet Others

Here are a few ways to meet those interested in the same thing: social networking. For example, you could explore the large number of paranormal-themed meetup.com groups around the country. There is bound to be one in your area or at least within driving distance. In fact, there may be more than one! Most meetup.com groups have regular public gatherings and events. A small fee is sometimes required to attend, especially if it is a public ghost hunt at a historic site that charges for investigative privilege (as most now do). Meetup.com also has message boards and membership directories. You can see who else is interested and even send private messages (members can specify settings regarding how much information is visible). The site is a great way to become familiar with other enthusiasts in your area without having to commit to a formally structured team.

You can also start to look up others in the paranormal community on Facebook or Twitter. Paranormal enthusiasts have always been social media savvy, a skill stemming from the Internet's early days. The community extensively engages social networking in all forms. Many well-known personalities have Facebook fan pages, and you can find others who participate in discussion boards on such sites.

What are other ways to find well-connected individuals? Do an Internet search for online paranormal radio shows; there are hundreds. In fact, it wouldn't surprise me if there aren't close to a thousand. Keep in mind that not all shows are created equally. Some online radio shows are not very informative at all. However, the more popular shows and Internet radio networks will have decent websites. Current credible shows include Darkness Radio (which explores all sorts of paranormal topics), and TAPS Family Radio. Online networks like Para-X Radio and Liveparanormal.com provide great content as well. Most shows are interactive, meaning they have a "chat" component where you can type with others listening to the show. This is another good way of getting information and networking. Search for podcasts of these types of shows, and you can decide which are best for you. These are excellent ways to learn too!

Another important way to meet others is through the discussion boards around the major shows or well-known groups. Ghostvillage .com, the TAPS main forum, and the TAPS 18+ forum are the largest online paranormal community message boards in the world. The Paranormal Research Society also has vibrant, active forums with useful information from a variety of learned sources. Likewise, the PRS regularly updates their sites with great stuff. Some local groups have their own forums, and this is also a good resource if such a team is in your area.

Local New Age stores often post (and sometimes host) paranormal-related events, assuming there are such shops in your area. If you have never been into a New Age bookstore, I understand it may feel strange to visit one. However, they offer many interesting things, and you will certainly run into open-minded people who may be able to point you in the right direction.

Finally, the most obvious course of action is to identify groups in your area and see if they need new members. Most groups announce on their website when they have available slots. Some groups are very informal and bring on new teammates after a quick email. Others may have you fill out a three-page questionnaire before they consider your participation.

Whatever the protocol, do not take any of it personally if you are not accepted to be on the team. Be forewarned that just because you may be very interested and there's a group in your area does not mean you'll get in. Sometimes they simply don't need an extra investigator. Other times, the team is looking for a specific type of person, perhaps someone with specialized skills. Some groups behave like social clubs and are very selective about whom they let in.

What to Look For

The growth of groups is now so widespread that you can find almost any personality type and social scenario. There are faith-based groups working off of religious principles, while others are scientific in approach. Some prioritize the use of psychics; others don't allow them in the team! As mentioned earlier, you need to know what you believe and why. If you do not believe in demons, then working with a faith-based group probably isn't your best choice.

It is wise for groups to put potential members through a vetting process. However, be cautious of teams that make huge claims or ask you to sign what you feel is unnecessary paperwork beyond standard confidentiality and liability. Confidentiality means that you won't divulge case information to anyone outside your team. Liability indicates the team is not responsible for what happens to you on group-related events, including while on investigation.

I've heard of a team that had members sign nondisclosure agreements, meaning they couldn't talk about anything or anybody in the group from now until the end of time, which is a bit fishy. It is important to stress that members keep cases confidential, but anything relating to personal behavior and your private life is absolutely uncalled for.

Also, watch for personal dynamics. Some teams function with the democracy concept, while others operate under little "dictatorships." It is always good to ask who makes the team's decisions: the founder, a few select few, or everyone? I'm not suggesting top-heavy power is always bad. Sometimes a strong, decisive leader is needed to get things off the ground. It is important, however, to know what you can deal with based on your personality type. You also need to be aware of any requirements for members. Some expect a minimum number of yearly investigations per team member, for example. Other groups expect regular participation on their forums, charity work involvement, and dues. Be prepared: group culture isn't just about doing an investigation. As I said earlier, there are strong social components to today's investigative culture.

A good friend pointed out that many ghost hunters today want to be dropped off at the door, have a few hours of fun, go home, and do nothing more. If you just want the experience, a serious group is not for you. Be honest about it and do investigations that won't require you to invest more time and energy than you have to give.

This may be the most important advice of all: be mindful that you are getting in with a reputable, tolerant group of people with whom you are comfortable. Look at their website. Does it look professional? Check out their evidence. Do you feel comfortable with what they are putting out there? Google the team and founder(s) names. A quick online search may let you know a bit more about who is involved and how the larger community perceives them. (But please, do not take it beyond a quick Internet search.) If you have any suspicions or discomfort, find another option.

No Groups?

If you are in an area where there is no formally organized community, you can start your own meetup.com or Facebook group. It is a great way to find others. This takes some money and funds—meetup.com does charge organizer dues of around $72 a year (monthly payments are accepted). Going this route also takes some decent organizational skills. But if you are seriously interested and have no other options, it is an easy thing to do. It is not recommended you post on craigslist; it is targeted to a general audience and you do not know what kinds of people will show up.

Facebook and Twitter are also becoming a popular place for area enthusiasts to organize. For starters, it is free to create a group on Facebook, and you can control permissions regarding how open the group is (for everyone or by invitation only). Facebook doesn't yet have the same features as meetup.com such as the calendar and user-friendliness, however. One disadvantage to Facebook is that your group feed may become indistinguishable from all the other groups and activities someone may have on his or her Facebook wall. It is also necessary to remain abreast of all setting and privacy changes that regularly occur with this social networking site.

Both of these resources have transformed paranormal interest, making it accessible and easy to organize. Many Facebook and meetup.com groups are managed by established teams who use the sites as ways to educate the public, share their research, and (sometimes) recruit new members. As such, they have become entry-level stops for many enthusiasts.

You can also visit online forums like Ghostvillage.com and TAPS 18+ and mention that you are looking for a team to join. Sometimes you run into the right people in your local area to make that happen.

Be Cautious

Here are a few things to consider when dealing with social networking-based groups. First, these things are open to the public, even if they are targeted to a particular interest group. Make sure you do not have any info out there you do not want publicly accessible such as home addresses and private numbers. Second, this subject area attracts some odd people at times. You have to use common sense when dealing with individuals you don't know very well (and this is true in any social setting). Finally, some meetup.com and Facebook group founders have become territorial in competing social networking efforts in the same geographical area. If you chose to start such a group or become a member of an already established area, it may not lead directly to membership in a team. Some in the community feel it has made dynamics even worse. Someone joins a meetup.com group, goes on a few public ghost hunts, and decides to start their own group in an area where there are already several preexisting groups. The truth is there are only so many haunted homes and historic sites that can accommodate all those wanting to "get cases."

Going It Alone

Many people—an increasing number, in fact—decide to bypass the complicated terrain of group management and dealing with paranormal community dynamics. Those who desire this normally want to have a good time or do real research.

Going it alone, however, is harder than it seems. The most successful freelancers are those who are already established or connected well enough that they can float around from one to team to another.

Investigation is currently a group-based endeavor. The secret to "freelancing" is to be unbiased, professional, and willing to work with everyone. You need to establish your reputation before groups will allow you to guest investigate with them. Getting to know people is one way to get in on cases. You also need to be willing to buy an assortment of equipment that makes your presence an asset on investigations. Additionally, you'll probably need to travel in order to work with a number of different teams.

When introducing yourself to teams, it is perhaps best to ask to meet, talk about ideas, and share information before you ask to come on an investigation. Attending local meetups and other events is a great way to meet people. Keep in mind that many groups are particular about whom they invite on their cases. Some of this is useless paranoia, and some of it is common sense. Nonetheless, freelancing is a great way to be exposed to a variety of personalities, techniques, and ideas. In many ways, it is more conducive to being part of a team, particularly if a team rarely networks and explores new concepts.

Another way is to go to paranormal conferences in whatever region of the country you live in. These are fun trips, and you get a chance to meet other like-minded individuals. TV personalities can sometimes show up too. It takes a little bit of money to go to these events, and you may not make contact with someone in your town. You can, however, start networking and get your name out there.

One emerging criticism of the team-based approach is that it limits information exchange and ideas. There are many paranormal networks around the world, the TAPS family being the most centrally organized global network of teams. However, American society is mobile; a perfectly good investigator can move to another town and be without a group, for example. He or she will be in a position to either foster new networks in the area (and this can be very complicated, considering community dynamics), or start a group from scratch, which may be problematic if there are already several teams in the area.

There are also plenty of potentially great investigators who for whatever reason cannot get on with a team due to a variety of reasons including philosophical and personality differences.

This is an important consideration: the nature of team-based culture often evolves around personalities. This is not true of all teams, but it is common for many that have emerged due to media influence. Personality-based teams operate around a "founder" mentality. Their long-term success is often compromised by drama, and such groups normally dissolve after a few years. Once again, good investigators may be in a situation where they have limited options once a group breaks up. Therefore, it is increasingly necessary for the paranormal community to move away from an exclusively team-based culture and focus more on creating a network of reputable individuals, even if they happen to belong to a team.

The International Paranormal Investigators does list both teams and individuals and may be a useful avenue for serious investigators to consider. If you are serious about learning and getting involved, these two networks are reputable and worth checking out. Troy Taylor's long-standing American Ghost Society is a paid organization that attracts serious individuals. Anyone can join; it is another wonderful way to meet really dedicated people.

There is a growing movement to support the concept of individual investigators working with everyone rather than only team-based investigation. There is still value in teamwork and group culture, but the field needs to relax to include diversity in research.

4: Starting a Group

You've made the decision to start your group! Congratulations, and be prepared for some work! I will outline the basic ways to get started. Keep in mind that the next section of the book details case management, so I won't cover that here.

I assume that you have a core group of people you trust and enjoy working with. Group dynamics can be very tricky. Here is a fact that many people may not share: you can have a group of perfectly reasonable, dedicated people who all have the same goal. However, it doesn't mean that everyone will be the right fit or get along. Your best friend may not necessarily be a great teammate.

Once you have a core group, you can decide how to formalize your team. Most groups formalize their existence in varying degrees. They come up with a name and design a website. I recommend an initial free site at wordpress.com or another blog site. It is one great way to get your presence out there, along with a Facebook page (which offers private discussion for select members). Keep in mind, however, that there remains a stigma with free websites—a hosted site and dedicated domain name expresses professionalism. But take baby steps in doing that until you know your group is running smoothly. In the meantime, a free website and content site such as Ning.com will do fine, the latter of which also offers forums for members. You can stipulate how much of the site's content is available for public view.

There are multiple ways to form a group, but I'll break it down into a few steps to help those who may need more help.

Decide Your Objective

Do you want to do this to have something to do on a weekend? Do you want your group to help concerned homeowners? Are you interested in doing more research-based investigation at historical locations? Want to just legend trip? (No shame in that!) Or maybe you feel called to help souls cross over. Decide the focus, and make sure everyone else is on the same page. Then write your mission statement.

Mission Statements

Your mission statement is important: it helps the public understand what you and your organization are about, and it also serves as a principle around which your group can organize. Here is a great mission statement from a group that likes to have fun while responsibly documenting their investigations at historical sites. If you want to legend trip, check out AdventureMyths:

> AdventureMyths investigates different locations locally, nationally, and internationally and discover if there is any validity to different myths, legends, and folklore. Data is compiled, all adventures and investigations are documented through video and audio, and a short documentary is created for viewers and listed on our YouTube page online.
>
> Some investigations have been published and full documentaries created for the establishment that was investigated. AdventureMyths's style of creating a documentary relies on personal accounts, history, and any

validated or unexplained phenomena captured by the group during film-
ing. Not only does the group enhance its research, we also are able to pro-
vide historical locations a product (DVD) they have the authority to re-
produce and sell, assisting in maintaining the property for years to come.

Although fun is one of the objectives, we at the same time try through
a realistic approach to see what truly exists in the world of the unknown.

In addition to our main mission, we also serve the general public
by educating them through video documentaries about the interesting
myths, legends, and folklore that surround us in our everyday lives.

Scientific Paranormal (SP) in upstate New York and Connecticut takes a different approach. SP is a family member of TAPS, and reflects the mission of many TAPS-family teams.

Scientific Paranormal is dedicated to providing scientific explana-
tions for claims of the paranormal in order to alleviate the fear and mis-
understanding of unknown events. Utilizing both advanced scientific
equipment and state-of-the-art software, Scientific Paranormal analyzes
evidence of the unexplained to solve claims of paranormal activity via
science and technology. Our continual mission is to provide answers and
scientific data for the scientific and public communities.

Given enough data to support our hypothesis and theories on para-
normal phenomena, Scientific Paranormal hopes to gain the ability to
accurately be able to show the differences between natural and unknown
phenomena. The scientific community will one day categorize this un-
known phenomena we hope.

Para Probers, founded by Reverend Sherrie James, provides a very nice mission statement for those who are spiritually based.

Our mission is to help anyone in need who is experiencing chal-
lenging haunts or who just needs someone to talk to about his or her
paranormal experiences. We are here to help any human—living or

dead—who might need our assistance or who just needs someone to listen.

Para Probers is a diverse, Christian faith-based team, but we accept clients from all faith backgrounds or those who hold no spiritual beliefs. Though we are spiritual, we also employ the highest standards for scientifically "probing" and evaluating our cases. We always search for natural explanations first. Para Probers is available to work with other paranormal investigation teams who are not prepared to handle negative cases or who just want some additional bodies on an investigation. We do accept referrals from other teams for negative cases or members will assist the team if they need clergy to conduct a house cleansing or blessing for their client. We enjoy learning from others, and we are open to sharing any information, techniques, or advice we have that might be helpful to other paranormal teams or individuals. We think that making new friends and networking is great! Please understand that we do respect the dead. We treat the dead with the same level of compassion as we do the living. Our team never provokes. We sincerely want to try to help any entity that needs it. We do not, however, believe that the rights of the dead or any negative entity should ever supersede the rights of the living.

All of these teams take vastly different approaches and their philosophy is reflected in their mission statements. Additionally, most teams always put in their mission that services are free of charge regardless of approach. Some groups do accept unsolicited donations from clients for gas and travel expenses and may include that in their mission.

Charging for an Investigation?

It is generally accepted that teams and individual investigators never charge for their services. There are many reasons for this. One is that it is difficult to adequately "prove" the existence of a ghost and even harder to remove a spirit or a haunting. This is not like a pest-control service. Paranormal research, likewise, is unregulated by a governing body, so anyone can investigate regardless of credentials or experience. This creates a potentially sticky legal situation should anyone charge.

Perhaps the biggest reason most contemporary investigators do not accept payment goes back to credibility issues. There is unfortunately a history of some who conducted ghost work exploiting desperate or frightened clients. Fraudulent mediums existed during Spiritualism's heyday and set an unfortunate standard for those who travel in the ghost frontier. Amateur paranormal investigators of the recent past sometimes demanded very high sums for investigations that sometimes included dubious psychic impressions. Today, it is generally considered highly unethical to ask for payment of any sort. In addition to the ethics of the matter, money exchange makes any situation potentially litigious.

However, there remain investigators today who charge several thousand dollars for investigation. These individuals are not a mainstream part of the paranormal community, but here is the thing—there are clients who are willing to pay even if there are reputable teams in their area who will investigate for free. It ultimately comes down to what someone is willing to do, and some individuals may feel a service is "better" if it requires a hefty fee. Someone will have a price tag as long as another is willing to pay. I personally feel that investigators who accept payment creates a sticky legal precedent for everyone should anything go wrong—say, a client sues because the activity continues, for example. That would change dynamics for all investigators if the court system got involved.

In a similar vein, there are also psychics who charge to visit haunted locations. These intuitives generally operate outside the ghost-hunting community. I cannot suggest that someone with psychic gifts should volunteer their time for no compensation, but I am aware that there are debates about this within the psychic community.

There are also paranormal researchers who charge to do private ITC sessions to help clients communicate with departed loved ones. This is also hotly contested, as many in the paranormal community consider ITC devices experimental technology.

It is essential to point out that paranormal research is a not-for-profit endeavor. In fact, be prepared to spend your own money if you want to ghost hunt. Investigators do acknowledge that rising gas costs and long-distance travel cut into personal budgets in big ways. Some groups state on their site that donations are appreciated but not required or necessary. Many teams are increasingly selective about what cases they accept based on distance and cost.

Online Presence

What you call your group and your mission statement is how you represent yourself to the world. Be mindful that what you name your group reflects how people perceive you. Reverend Sherrie James started a faith-based group called Para Probers. She suggests, "Finding the right name is very important and difficult, especially considering so many names are already taken! You want a name that reflects what you do." She settled on Para Probers because "it adequately reflected what we do; we probe into the paranormal."

Don't go with a name similar to other known groups in your area. It is tacky and shows you have not done any research. Also, don't give yourself a clichéd name unless you want to project that image. I know of a small group that called themselves "Ghoul Chasers." They may have been great folks, but a few local historic sites didn't feel comfortable with that kind of thing.

Establish some type of online presence and post your mission statement with general information about your team. It is also advisable to put member names (or at least first names) and a photo. This helps any potential clients and locations identify with you. It also builds a relationship of trust, and serves as a good security measure so clients know in advance who is coming on to their property. Of course, some investigators may not desire to have their identity out in the open for professional reasons.

Also, make sure anyone visiting the site knows how to contact you. Please do yourself a favor and refrain from putting a private telephone number on the site—for your own security and sanity. There are people who will call you at 2 a.m. to tell you there is a ghost at the end of the bed at that very moment. Trust me—it gets old. A Skype number is inexpensive and unintrusive. Google Voice is also increasingly popular as the service is free (at the time of this writing) and includes voicemail and call forwarding. Actually, email will do just fine for initial contact.

Please take extra care to make sure there are no grammatical or spelling mistakes on your site; they reflect poorly on you, your group, and the field at large.

Some teams form and then immediately want to design logos and purchase T-shirts and other related accessories. Having team T-shirts is great but there seems to be considerable emphasis put into the need for some sort of uniform. This is not an initial requirement although I *will* recommend that you come up with a basic dress code that includes sensible shoes and professional, comfortable attire. I discuss these things later when we get to protocol.

Yet if you insist on building team morale with your own T-shirt, cafepress and Vistaprint are two online sources for team-logo inspired gear. Vistaprint and Zazzle.com also offer inexpensive business cards. You can upload a logo at any of the above sites and have it printed on a variety of items, including car magnets.

Team Paperwork

It is essential for teams to have several documents protecting their interests and those of the client. The first document most teams have is a confidentiality and liability waiver for team members. This document absolves the team from assuming responsibility for any injuries or accidents occurring during investigation or team-related events. A confidentiality agreement may also be created, which is a document stating that you are bound as a team member not to share client or case information outside the team. Likewise, you will not "poach" cases by handing clients over to other area teams.

Another piece of paperwork involves the client and releasing him or her from any responsibility should you hurt yourself while on their property. Well-worded documents may also protect the organization from being liable should something occur.

Some groups extend paperwork and investigator contracts to include what they will and will not do as a team. For one, most groups do not charge clients. Second, some groups will not guarantee to rid a haunting or to cross a spirit over; they have a client sign paperwork in acknowledgment. If a group does specific things like ghost cleansing, those also need to be stipulated in the document. Always have two copies available—one for you and one for the client.

Finally, a confidentiality agreement between team and client is very important. However, because it gets into case management issues, we'll save that for when we discuss case management.

Having a paper trail detailing all expectations and agreements is essential but here is the reality: it is hard to enforce any contracts unless your organization is a registered nonprofit or if the forms are notarized. There is some debate regarding how legally solvent these documents are if a group is not a registered nonprofit, corporation, or limited liability company. Don't let this dissuade you from preparing solid paperwork, however. It is important to stress ethics from the beginning, and having a paper trail is necessary for both you and clients.

Background Checks

I put this section under paperwork because it is essential for any potential investigator to divulge a criminal record on paper, and it is well within your rights to ask a person to do so. You also have the right to conduct background checks, but you must reveal that you are doing so. Laws may differ from state to state on this matter, but it is ethical to let anyone know if you plan to conduct a criminal check.

TAPS family teams and most reputable groups require basic background checks on team members. Most protocol will exclude accepting any individual convicted of a felony. After all, you are going into private homes (sometimes with children present) and historic sites with your clients' trust to behave ethically. It is unnerving for clients to later realize a felon may have been on his or her property, particularly if that person was charged with a violent crime or is a sex offender.

I am not suggesting that individuals with a felony record are always bad news; sometimes people go through difficult and unfortunate periods of their lives where bad decisions were made. It does not mean that individuals with criminal records cannot play a part on a team, but it *does* mean that team founders and case managers should use discretion on these matters.

It is OK to ask any potential members to sign paperwork indicating the likelihood of a background check and ask them at that time to voluntarily divulge any past criminal history (traffic tickets and most misdemeanors are excluded). Likewise, these things should remain confidential and not be shared with other team members.

Drug testing is generally not part of vetting individuals for team membership. For one thing, it costs money (background checks do, as well). The prevailing idea is what one does with their personal time is personal. However, most team protocol explicitly bans the use of recreational drugs and alcohol during investigations and will ask investigators to confidentially share with the case manager or team founder if he or she is on any prescription medications that may alter behavior during the investigation. The same can be said if any investigator has a medical condition that may interfere with his or her ability to investigate.

It is generally accepted that investigators going through unusual and profound emotional and psychological stress should refrain from going on out investigation, depending on the context. The following form from IN*sight* Paranormal provides an example of a Member Liability form, which should be signed by all members and guest investigators.

Sample Team Member Liability Form

IN*sight* Paranormal, based out of Oklahoma City, has a wonderfully well-written example of a basic member liability form. Here is how it is worded (and feel free to borrow and make it your own):

I, _____, will be participating in various events as a member of [group name]. I recognize that instances of investigations of locations and property can be dangerous if not approached properly. I also recognize that certain investigations may be held on undeveloped land that often cannot be made safe. Further, I recognize that certain investigations may be physically strenuous and/or emotionally unsettling.

I assume the risk for any injuries that I may sustain while participating in the events as a member of [group name].

In consideration for being allowed to join [group name,] and participate in various events, including investigations, I release and forever discharge from [group name] and all of its members, officers, and directors from any actions, suits, damages, claims, or judgments that may result from any personal injury I may sustain while engaged in any and all events I participate in as a member of [group name].

[Group name] does not carry or subscribe to any form or type of health, accident, or bodily injury insurance. By signing below, I acknowledge [group name] does not have any form of insurance for its members and that I am required to maintain health insurance as a precondition to my participation in group events.

I have read, understand, and agree to be bound by the terms of this document. This release of liability shall be effective for the duration of my membership in [group name].

In witness whereof, I have executed this release at _____ (location of execution) on _____ (date).

_____
Signature of member

_____
Signature of Witness/[group name] Cofounder

Formalizing Your Group

Many groups function just fine as grassroots, volunteer-based organizations. It is easy to manage, and there's no great loss should the group disband. Let us be realistic: sometimes life just gets in the way and it becomes hard to maintain interest, regardless of how much we care about investigation.

But suppose you are part of a group that has been around for a year or more. Now may be time for the next step: becoming a formal organization. A logical and popular step is to become a registered nonprofit in your state. Each state has a slightly different process, so you will need to find out how to do this. It can be lengthy depending on where you live and requires proper documentation. Normally, it involves paperwork and putting together a board of directors. Getting nonprofit status means you are a legal corporation and that you can legally fundraise or ask for tax-deductible donations.

The nonprofit process is a good one to undertake, but it can be time consuming. Some groups are now looking at becoming limited liability companies or purchasing bond insurance. All of these are good steps if your group becomes serious and appears to have staying power. However, there is time, money, and resources invested in going down these routes so think carefully before deciding to do so.

Most groups do not have the resources to consult lawyers on these matters, but it is a good idea to do a little bit of legal homework to make sure the language is appropriate and reflects whatever state requirements are necessary. Again, the level of paperwork depends on what type of investigation you are doing.

Thinking About Protocol

Most groups come up with some basic protocol and "rules." This takes time to manage. Some rules may be as simple as not showing up to an investigation intoxicated or not wearing perfume. Most groups point out designated smoking areas during investigation, as smoke can appear as anomalies on video and photograph. These things are more often about good manners than real research protocol.

Yes, good manners are important. Personal hygiene and cleanliness are essential, as well as a neat appearance. Dress code should reflect comfort and practicality. Team members should refrain from wearing sexually provocative clothing or profanity-laced graphic T-shirts, for example. I would go far as to avoid any T-shirts that advocate personal political or religious beliefs, particularly if you are going into private homes.

For safety reasons, women need not wear high heels or impractical shoes on investigation. Most protocol will insist that investigators remove sparkly jewelry and avoid donning perfume or cologne so that phantom smells are not confused with any store-bought personal fragrances (and out of consideration for others, as not everyone can tolerate such smells). Deodorant is always appreciated, but sometimes investigators do get smelly after a whole night of crawling through old haunted sites. Consider it a bonding experience!

There is more detailed protocol beyond manners and dress that a good team needs to outline. For example, you may want to be clear about how the team needs to handle EVP work. One may suggest that during EVP sessions, all investigators must pause 15–30 seconds between questions. You may also have other procedural elements in place regarding investigators being alone a room. Some teams say investigators must never be alone, while others will deem it OK if the investigator is within earshot of others or if other additional audio and video equipment is present to make sure any evidence captured is legitimate.

I recommend writing these out and making protocol a living document, meaning that it can change as you learn over time what works for you and your team. Here is some protocol that may be useful for you:

• At least one team member must enter the location "hot"—
  meaning they have audio and/or video on from the moment
  they leave the car on a location, even before setup takes place.

This idea comes from Paul Browning, who always uses this technique because he has found the most intriguing personal events occur the moment video and audio are turned off! HNC has one member keep a digital audio recording until they are in the car when leaving a case.

- Investigators must tag all noises during investigation, including stomach growls, loud sighs, and other environmental events. This includes if someone inadvertently passes gas, as well. It can be embarrassing but it is necessary.

- Investigators must not whisper during the investigation. I know that we see this done on TV but it is not supposed to happen.

- One investigator must be responsible for photography during sessions.

- One investigator must have a reliable EMF detector on hand during sessions.

The above are basic protocol examples present in many teams. Protocol is normally quite extended.

One protocol example I want to share is adapted from something similar used by the Windbridge Institute during EVP work. This is very a regimented approach for EVP work but one that may be useful for your team, modified as you see fit.

A group of four people are in a room at a haunted location. Each person has a distinct role to play during EVP sessions:

- One person monitors the camera.

- One person asks EVP questions. There is a certain time allotted between questions. All others in the room have mouth guards in to prevent them from speaking.

- One person jots down all environment noises during EVP session.

- All members are in front of the camera at all times with the exception of the one watching the monitor.

This type of EVP work is tedious and methodological, but it is specifically designed to rule out most false positives and criticisms against any captured evidence. The idea of wearing mouth guards seems extreme but it does help buffer skeptics if an EVP emerges during such controlled sessions.

Again, your protocol depends on your objective. Faith-based teams may insert religious protocol, while scientific teams will engage methodology in a different way.

Finally, well-established teams have handbooks for all members so they know where the group stands on certain issues, expected protocol, and evidence review and data management. It takes some time to come up with protocol, and it is often a work in progress.

Money—The Real Story

Let me spell this out. If you want to be part of a team, expect to pay at least $500 a year. Any hobby, from tennis to gaming, will run you at least this much. Paranormal investigation is no different.

It is unnecessary to have thousands of dollars' worth of equipment like we see on TV, but ghost hunting is not cheap. Here's what any serious hobbyist or researcher needs:

First, you will need sufficient money to pay for gas to go on investigations. Rising gas prices make this an issue, particularly if haunt jaunts are frequently out of town. Throw in the cost of the occasional dinner eaten before or after an investigation as well. Reverend James noted that increasing gas prices has forced her to alter protocol for her group, as "it is much harder for people to go to investigations outside of the local area."

One also needs a reliable vehicle or very supportive friends who can help transport you to an investigation. This seems obvious, but I have encountered several situations where unreliable transportation seriously impeded the ability for individuals to be a meaningful part of a group.

Be prepared to pay for investigations at most historic sites, which have now realized paranormal interest is profitable. Large, well-known locations often charge $700–$1000 per group (meaning ten people or more, so perhaps $100 each) to investigate all night. Smaller, lesser-known locations may charge a few hundred or per head. It is easier for groups to investigate these sites as residential cases may not be easily accessible. Therefore, it is conceivable that one needs several hundred dollars to invest annually just towards investigating historic locations.

Groups often ask for membership dues to help with maintaining a website, buying T-shirts, and other group-related management tasks. Most dues are very affordable. Be prepared to honor financial requirements so the obligation is split evenly among the members.

One also needs to be able to invest at least a few hundred dollars in buying basic equipment. This means a reputable digital audio recorder with quality earphones for EVP review (not ear buds). There are some other basic items, such as an EMF detector; handheld camcorders are extremely useful. One does not have to purchase the top-of-the-line expensive items, but one can realistically expect to invest an initial $500 in buying the basics. This includes batteries, camcorder mini-DV tapes or extra memory cards for storage, even a small first aid kit for the car, and other incidentals that can add up quite quickly.

Please understand that very few groups provide members with equipment. While well-established teams may be able to supplement members with some equipment, investigators are expected to purchase personal items in order to be part of a team.

It is not necessary to go buy a new computer for ghost hunts, but you need to make sure the computer you have can manage audio/video file transfer and running the software needed for this. Notebooks are more common than ever and are great for doing casual Internet surfing and word processing, but these devices are not able deal with large amounts of data. Most higher-end laptops and desktops are fine. You need a computer with working USB ports and memory to install video and audio editing software if your computer doesn't already have it. An external hard drive is necessary if you do a large number of cases—those video and audio files take up a lot of space! I understand this seems obvious, but some are not computer-savvy enough to consider these things.

Of course, there are many enthusiasts who just want to enjoy an occasional ghost hunt. In that case, they invest a great deal of money in going to conferences or other events where they can do public investigation. For these, a good digital audio recorder, a camera, and a flashlight are the basics.

A notebook and pen are important for any investigator. Likewise, one can also audio tag any significant events for later review (this is my preferred method, by the way, as carrying around an extra paper pad is cumbersome). Tablet computers are also emerging as very useful ways to document what happens while on investigation, particularly for note taking.

Starter Equipment

As I just pointed out, serious investigators have to purchase decent basic equipment. What I feel you need is a good EMF detector, a good quality digital audio recorder that can record in .wav format, and a camcorder with night vision or an IR illuminator. All the other gadgets, like K-II meters, ghost boxes, laser grids, and that other stuff are fun but not necessary for beginners—or even useful for seasoned investigators.

You can purchase camcorders and digital audio devices at most big-box stores. There are ghost gear sites online as well. We will get into the nitty-gritty of equipment in another chapter.

You'll need suitable way to protect and transport your gear. I am low-tech and use a laundry basket (hey, it works). Other people buy specialized cases. Regardless of your motivations, learn how to use your equipment.

Something to Know:
Additional Items That May Come in Handy

- Toilet tissue, wet wipes, hand sanitizer

- GPS

- Small first aid kit

- Batteries—lots of them

- Screwdrivers (various sizes and heads) in order to change batteries on your equipment

- A hunting vest or tool belt may be useful to hold gear while you are out on investigation

- Extension cords, power cords, and duct tape are always important

5: Team and Case Structure

So you've got a few people together and you're ready to go. The biggest challenge for any new investigator or team is landing cases.

Cases are essential. The way investigators work is they go to places and investigate. It sounds obvious, but it can be a daunting chore for new groups. Getting cases is now complicated by the fact that most areas have several teams and there are only so many local sites one can approach. Keep in mind that very well-known locations have already been hit up for investigation. If you want to investigate, you and every other person in your team need to make an active (and legal) effort to find cases.

What Not To Do

First, the obvious thing to point out is do not EVER do anything illegal or unethical in efforts to get a case, including trespassing. Someone owns every site and abandoned cemetery, even if it's not immediately obvious. Paranormal investigation is so popular that someone has probably investigated unknown little backwoods cemeteries at this point. Make sure you have permission to be wherever you go.

There is a well-known incident that occurred in North Carolina of a team illegally train-spotting for a notorious "ghost train." They did not have permission to be there, and foolishly did not check the train schedules beforehand. They thought the vibrating tresses were an incoming phantom train. Sadly, it was the real thing, and a few investigators did not get off the tracks in time. The other investigators, knowing they did not have permission to be there, fled the site. One investigator was badly injured while another lost his life. This is an extreme yet real example of how irresponsibility can be deadly. Likewise, the person who died was probably a decent investigator and a good guy, but he will forever be remembered for this particular act.

Loyd Auerbach related an occurrence in California where a team went to a certain neighborhood and just knocked on doors at private homes they "felt" might be haunted. We've all passed properties that look enticing, but this type of behavior is invasive, irresponsible, and unethical.

Many teams badly want to land that first case—or any case. Social networking sites like Facebook and Twitter often make it easy to see what locations other local groups are investigating, particularly if home owners post on Facebook feeds in efforts to get help from a particular team. If the location is public, there is no harm in approaching the site. However, please do not poach cases from other teams. It doesn't matter if you see a homeowner post on another team's wall or if you hear about a case through the grapevine.

Such things happen more than one may realize. Some groups work with other teams, then go behind their backs and approach clients or locations to let them in as well. Here is some advice: don't troll social networking sites or the rumor mill undermining other teams. The best way to get cases is to be in good standing with the larger paranormal community who will work with you or refer clients. Acting unprofessional is a surefire way for you and your team to not go very far.

Just Getting Practice

As you wait for cases, you may be itching to go out and do a ghost hunt. You have your new camera or digital audio recorder and are ready to go! In the meantime, it is good to get some practice in. The question is, where?

Some cemeteries and graveyards are open to paranormal investigation. There are differing opinions on just how "haunted" such sites are. Some feel they are a gold mine for activity, while others suggest intelligent haunts occur at places the dead found meaningful while alive. People aren't buried until they have been dead for several days. Regardless, some cemeteries appear to be active and remain great places to do some trial runs. Anyone can go to cemeteries during the day, assuming they are publicly accessible. Just be sure you have permission to be at such sites after hours. Of course, respect the property and the families of those buried there. Cemeteries not attached to churches may prove easier for obtaining permission.

You do not have to go places at night, despite what you may see on TV. Honestly, paranormal activity happens all the time. It is just more convenient for some to investigate in the evening because they are not at work. Likewise, homeowners are more likely to notice activity at night because it is when they are home.

Taking tours of historic locations with your digital audio recorder or camcorder (depending on what is allowed) in hand is another way to get some basic practice under your belt. Obviously there will be noise contamination, and any evidence you collect is subject to scrutiny. I know investigators who have obtained potential EVP during such tours. Several people have claimed to capture EVP during public hours at Körner's Folly, for example. The value in this is getting practice downloading, listening, and working with audio and video files.

Of course, you can spend the money to attend some organized paranormal events that offer investigations with well-known personalities.

These investigations are not "real" investigations, but they do offer you a chance to hone your skills and equipment at haunted sites.

Your best bet is to "rent" out a historic location as so many now offer after-hours access for paranormal investigation. However, certain locations may have requirements and will most likely ask for some type of fee or donation. You have to weigh your resources, desires, and motivations as a new group before deciding to sink money into getting an investigation somewhere. The joy of this is that you may not need an official group to get into certain places; you may just need a group of interested friends who can pitch in to cover the cost. There are benefits to haunted road-tripping!

If your motivation is to learn, you may want to consider some organized educational events. TAPS Academy, launched in 2011, is an intensive lecture and investigation course occurring at various sites around the country. These lecture series go beyond the TAPS approach and brings in parapsychology, quantum physics, consciousness studies, and some esoteric elements. It is another great way to learn, meet others, and get some investigative experience under your belt.

The Paranormal Research Society has offered online courses in the past for a very reasonable cost. The courses are organized around a topic, such as historical overviews of research or evidence analysis. Online courses may not offer investigation experience but they do provide a good way to learn. A few times a year, the PRS also sponsors "field trips" at various haunted sites around the country. These events provide educational and investigative opportunities, as well as a chance to socialize with some PRS members.

In the beginning, I just wanted to jump in and get my feet wet. I can appreciate a newbie's enthusiasm and eagerness to just go ghost hunting. So how do you do it if you don't have anywhere to go? You can always practice in your home. There are differing opinions on that, as well. Some are fine doing a "protocol practice" even if a home isn't active just to go through the motions and learn how to use equipment. Others feel this is blurring the boundaries a bit too much, fearing one can conjure or call something up. Many ITC enthusiasts suggest that one does not need to go to a haunted location to work with these devices, for example, which suggests that spirits or energies can come to you.

I cannot say either way if investigation opens portals or doors in and of itself. I do not like investigating in my home because I do not have activity, nor do I want to take a chance. I have played around with my equipment in my house, however. Take your EMF detectors, turn your microwave on, and stand in front of it. You'll see how your EMF gauge reacts. Put it up to the refrigerator, fuse box, or wireless router. Slowly walk away to see how far the EMF field extends. See how your gadgets response to normal, everyday appliances. You can learn a great deal just doing normal stuff with your equipment.

My kid thoroughly enjoyed turning the microwave on and off with the EMF in hand. When I got my IR digital thermometer, he stood over the stove to measure the heat of food while I cooked. I never knew beef stew could get so hot!

Here's a basic reality: most early cases come through word of mouth, and simply asking around may yield a great location. Again, those first cases do not have to be necessarily haunted. You want the chance to see how your team works together, how comfortable you are with equipment, and some experience reviewing evidence. Then, at some point, the cases do start coming in. Then the game changes.

Before we get to real case work, however, I want to state that I know people move at different speeds. They may want to approach the ghost frontier a bit differently than I do, for example. There are some out there who are called to legend trip.

Legend Tripping—Just for Fun!

There are many people who just want to go out and have a good time and a cool experience. To be honest, all ghost hunters want to have a cool experience. We would love to have ghostly events on investigation every five minutes, but that is not how it works, unfortunately.

The legend tripping concept comes from anthropology and folklore studies. It once referred to a teenage rite of passage. Jeff Belanger borrowed the term to basically refer to the pursuit of stories. One need not have a team or even fancy equipment to go out and pursue legends. Travel Channel's *Ghost Adventurers* team (which does have awesome equipment), has personified the legend tripping position. It is no accident that Jeff is a researcher and writer for the show.

Some in the ghost-hunting community take great offense to the legend tripping philosophy, suggesting that it is almost unethical. Their opinion is that going out to collect data or stories is invasive to the spirits we seek. It is hard to know exactly what ghosts or spirits may think or feel. What I will suggest is that if someone just wants to go out and have a fun ghost hunt—let that person be a proud legend tripper. These people have their own role to play and what they do most often does not involve going into a client's home. As I have suggested, those cases are for different types of investigators.

Legend tripping does require basic ethics and responsibilities, however. Do not trespass or mistreat property or people involved in your legend tripping. You should still have professional etiquette when approaching individuals or locations. One reason legend tripping gets a potentially bad rap in the paranormal community is because some people who take this approach behave quite badly. One does not need a formal group to legend trip. In fact, Jeff suggests the beauty of it is that it needs to remain relaxed; it is about fun and about engaging local stories!

If you want to legend trip in an effective way, you still go through the same procedures as a group looking for cases. You have to find and secure sites. There are witnesses to interview, and you'll need to keep some record of this.

Most paranormal teams' work is claim-based, meaning there is some sort of claims to justify an investigation. Legend tripping, however, allows you to carry on without specific reports. All you need is a good story—even better if there are claims attached! For example, you do not need a haunted house to legend trip. All you need is a bridge with a haunted story, or a railroad track with an attached legend (just be mindful that you aren't on the tracks when a train approaches). You still may want to interview people about their experiences and feelings about a location, which helps you tell your own story. Chris Balzano and Jeff Belanger, prolific authors of paranormal related books, use the example of phantom hitchhiker. It is hard to actually investigate these stories from a scientific perspective unless you can be at a location night after night, but you can certainly flesh out the story by interviewing those who have heard from a friend who heard from a friend… see what I mean?

There is some value in legend tripping many hardcore paranormal investigators fail to see. This approach really demonstrates the importance of how story relates to hauntings. Balzano writes, "These myths have had a collective effect on our culture. The story becomes a haunting in and of itself. There are no firsthand witnesses to the haunting but rather a character…" To a degree, all case claims and clients are telling a story that is linked up to larger emotional and cultural issues. Paranormal investigation is often about making a homeowner feel less haunted and by offering some sort of resolution, if possible. Legend tripping is not about resolving a haunting; it is about keeping the story alive.

I believe that legend tripping is also about your own role in that story. The most effective way to do this is through video documentation. AdventureMyths provides a great, high-end example of this. They used to be client-based investigators but wanted something more (hey, we are all called in different ways). Over rum in an Irish castle, they decided they wanted to start legend tripping at historic locations. They desired to document their investigation, do historical research, and then put together a media product to give back to the site. They are emerging as some of the most prolific legend trippers in the ghost hunting community. And they happen to be ethical, responsible investigators. They take the research seriously, but they also have fun with it. Adventure-Myths decided they wanted to use investigation as a way to tell a location's unique story. After all, we are all born storytellers!

Landing Those First Cases

You may or may not be a legend tripper, but all those in the ghost frontier desire cases. Getting a case is fairly easy if you approach public sites known for being haunted. Many known haunted sites open to investigation although they normally request a donation or fee. There are some in the paranormal community who feel it is wrong for sites to charge. The truth is, you are basically renting out a location for a "special event" at very inconvenient hours. Plus, historic sites appreciate all the funds they can get! It is a good idea to know where the funds are going—in some instances, the fee goes straight into someone's pocket. I would rather my money go directly to help the property, but that is my own personal opinion. You can always ask historic sites for a receipt as many locations are registered nonprofits and any donation is tax-deductible.

In soliciting cases, I cannot express how important it is to write clear, grammatically correct emails. You want to demonstrate credibility, and poorly written emails compromise that. I have had personal conversations with historic site managers who have refused investigations to groups with unprofessional email requests because "it was hard to take them seriously."

A case solicitation to a well-known location looks something like this:

> *Hello. My name is _____. I am a member of _____ (group) based in (your city here). We are aware that this location is available for paranormal investigation. We are interested in exploring*

the opportunity to investigate this property. Please let us know of any
requirements and stipulations involved in requesting an investigation.
      Here is the link to our group (and provide the site).
      Thank you for your consideration. I look forward to hearing from you.

You can add previous public sites that you have investigated, or you can say that you are a new team and "appreciate the opportunity to train" at this location. Be honest and upfront.

Once a site responds, you can then request several potential dates for investigation—and be willing to alter those dates based on availability. Be clear about how long you have permission to remain at the property. Also, get in writing whatever payment is required and find out if funds are needed in advance or paid upon arrival.

Keep in mind that the person organizing the investigation may be responsible for paying if other members don't do so—this could be a big problem, as some sites require funds up front. Make sure there are no misunderstandings, and impress upon members that they need to pay you in advance if required.

Most locations require you to sign a waiver or paperwork for legal and/or insurance purposes. This is normal. Some sites may require you to return a report or any evidence within a certain time frame. Again, each site differs. Make sure you understand all the requirements and stipulations beforehand, and please honor them.

Finally, accept that some locations, no matter how spooky they look, aren't going to let you in. Ever. Do not take it personally. There are many places that are paranormal-friendly, but some locations remain uninterested for personal, philosophical, or very practical reasons. Fort Fisher, a place in North Carolina, no longer allows investigations due to previous teams' misbehavior. If a location isn't interested, thank them for their time and move on.

Your Team and Organizational Responsibilities

Since *Ghost Hunters*, many teams have emulated the TAPS organizational model, meaning there is a founder, lead investigator, tech person, researcher, and so on. Teams are often top-heavy, meaning they are focused around a founding personality who has invested personal time and income into getting the group off the ground.

The TAPS model is one way to work but it isn't the only way to run a group. There are multiple models, but one thing is for sure: diverse people bring in different skills, and a team can be a learning opportunity for everyone. As HNC has an experienced historian, it makes sense that he does the bulk of historical research, but it also follows that others learn from this person how to do it themselves.

Team structure often depends on the resources and needs of your team. It is not always necessary to fit individuals into one role. In reality, most investigators will play multiple roles.

Here are a few key components that need to be fleshed out in any group. I prefer to look at these elements as potential "committees" rather than individual responsibilities:

- *Case Management:* This involves the initial client contact that comes in through email or phone. Cases management is generally involved in setting up cases and making sure the entire investigative process is followed through. Some may have less formal roles. A "lead investigator" may take this role but the responsibilities are the same.

- *Research:* This includes historical and scientific research, and literature review. The historical is an obvious component, but the scientific aspect is often under-utilized. Also, literature review is necessary. For example, some team members can be responsible for learning about place memory (residual) haunts or any given topic in order to be more informed about certain cases.

- *Equipment/Technical:* This isn't just about developing cool equipment (it can be) or purchasing the latest gadget (what fun!). This is about having a group of people responsible for knowing how to use equipment, troubleshooting, having fresh batteries, and so on. In reality, investigators should know how to use their own equipment regardless of who is "tech" person and should have their own batteries in their pocket. However, this role is useful if there are investigators able to develop prototype or experimental tools or troubleshoot.

- *Investigators:* These are individuals who actually do fieldwork, but many are involved with actual investigation. Not all team members may do this. Some may do case management or help the organization run on a daily basis. Fieldwork means knowing how to manage equipment, ideas, thoughts, hypotheses, events, and behavior while on investigation.

- *Noninvestigative Support:* Some groups have fundraisers, public relations people, broadcast technicians, and external consultants. Some team members may review evidence or do case management rather than fieldwork. All teams benefit from some type of noninvestigative support and provide an opportunity for good people to participate who may not be able to go on haunt jaunts very often. Having specialized roles like a media person is fine if your group grows in that direction. Take it slow in the beginning, and make sure to cover the basics per your objective.

6: Residential Cases— Not for Everyone

Let me be frank: Residential cases are not for everyone. This area is becoming one of increasing concern: there are a number of teams who go into private homes and mistreat the client, fake evidence, or simply don't know how to manage a situation. When I say "a situation," I don't mean the activity, although sometimes that is the case. As I discussed earlier, the media influence has made it rather trendy for people to be "haunted." In some cases, paranormal phenomena are occurring. In other cases, there are very real emotional and psychological issues going on that few in the paranormal community can legally treat or diagnose. It is imperative that one is very careful in dealing with any private home cases.

Some investigators want to help people because they themselves need to feel important. There are individuals who feel called to assist people, and often these individuals have personally had to deal with paranormal events in their own lives. If you do decide to help people, please be honorable and ethical. Please do not use "helping clients" as a way to work through your own insecurities or feelings of low self-esteem. Ouch! It hurts me to write that sentence as much as it will hurt some people to read it, but it is part of the mix. Here is a good adage to live by: do no harm.

There are also increasingly serious legal issues at hand. What if something goes missing during an investigation? Your team may be at fault, even if no one touched anything. I have heard of historic locations requiring teams to take pictures of every single speck of space before an investigation as a way to inventory valuables.

Sometimes you investigate places that are structurally weird. What if someone falls down the stairs during investigation? There are certainly liability forms that everyone must have, but there are so many other considerations that must be dealt with. Finally, what if you leave and the client claims activity actually worsens? This situation happens often, as we do not always understand the reasons for a haunting. It isn't always because a "bad" team went in, although unethical teams do make things worse, at least emotionally, for residential clients.

I hate being a downer, but these are complex issues that an increasing number of groups and investigations are forcing the community to consider.

It is hard for new groups to get residential cases; there are many groups present in most areas. The best way to start is to investigate a friend's house or someone you know. An online presence helps bring people to you, as does getting your name out there. The reality is there are many groups in any given area and only a limited supply of haunted private residences.

If other teams get to know you, they may refer cases to you if you are closer. But treat clients right. Be polite. Wear clean socks on investigation in case a client asks you to remove your shoes. Have a neat appearance. Don't smoke inside their homes. Ask before you use the restroom.

Don't pry in their personal belongings. Reach out to other groups. Show your professionalism and eventually, cases will come.

One big question to ask before deciding to take any residential case is this: How can our team best help a client with their situation, regardless of the potential presence of paranormal activity? This is an important question but one many teams overlook because they are equipped only to deal with a ghost—many have no idea how assist a client if there are other ongoing issues. In fact, some groups want there to be a ghost so badly that they may overlook other obvious variables contributing to the situation.

Client Rights

One of the most important emerging ethical issues is the idea of client rights. Much attention is focused on waiver, liability, and other information, but here's the deal: people are bringing you into their homes—their private spaces—and sharing things with you they may be afraid to tell anyone else. Honor the trust.

I hadn't had many serious, urgent cases until I started writing this book. Most residential cases I had experienced, in all honesty, had more of a party atmosphere, to a degree. The investigation was serious, of course, but these particular cases had curious clients rather than frightened ones. In fact, one reveal was like a mini family reunion. The client, a widower, had invited his entire family and neighbors, and had drinks and snacks available. The situation was bittersweet; we believed that we collected evidence from his departed wife. That case was happy and celebratory.

It isn't always like that, however. One case I worked on dealt with a military family: a deployed husband, his wife, and small children. The wife was so frightened by events in her home that she ended up leaving on occasions. She once left so quickly in her fright that a dirty diaper was left on the living room couch.

We investigated her home but didn't find any solid evidence. A clergy member came in and performed two blessings, but the activity allegedly continued. The client was genuinely scared, and the situation was truly baffling. This was no party atmosphere at all, and it feels horrible not to be able to empower a client. Unfortunately, one cannot always decipher the mysteries or provide what a client needs, regardless of how professional one may be.

This incident helped me realize that some cases take a very serious emotional toll on clients and investigators. There are moments when a family does not know where else to turn and sometimes reluctantly reaches out to a paranormal group. Then, in return, investigators invest time, money, and emotional energy into helping. This part of investigation is absolutely no joke. I have said this before—these cases are not meant for everyone, and some investigators are ill-suited for such work.

Therefore, honoring that responsibility is essential, and the basic rules are very simple. Be polite before, during, and after an investigation. Keep your client informed regarding how long it may take you to review evidence. Update him or her if evidence review takes longer than expected. Always send a final report and follow up with the client to discuss the findings or any lack thereof.

One of the most important elements is to respect a client's wishes regarding confidentiality. HNC has three levels of confidentiality for clients to determine. They are:

- HNC has the right to use and distribute all evidence obtained from the investigation, including the location where evidence was captured (note: we never list addresses, however, and this normally refers to nonresidential locations).

- HNC has limited use, meaning it may post evidence but cannot reveal where or when the evidence was captured.

- HNC has no rights to use the evidence in any form except for confidential reports between HNC and client.

I feel this provides adequate room for clients to control what they want shared or not.

Another issue is how soon the client can expect follow-up from the team's investigation. Clients have a right to a report, at a bare minimum, even in the absence of any evidence. A report (and sample reports are included later in this book) demonstrates the lengths a team has gone to in attempts to document or debunk claims of activity.

Clients also have other rights, as outlined by United Paranormal International with help from Loyd Auerbach. A client's religious preference must always be respected. Likewise, clients have the right to know the religion of all investigators in attendance, if asked. Clients are never to be judged or ridiculed based on ethnicity, educational level, economic class, sexual orientation, living conditions, personal beliefs, or appearance.

Investigators also have certain rights. They have the right to ask clients to lock away all firearms, valuables, and pets during the investigation. Likewise, investigators have the right to expect the client not to do anything to impede or disrupt the investigation or to deliberately create an unsafe environment.

7: Managing Your Cases

So, you finally have a case! How do you break it down to make it manageable and get the most out of it for you and your client?

Case management is really the neck of the investigative side of your group. It is the front and back end, so to speak, as it involves the initial client contact and often the final reveal. Groups are organized differently; my perspective may not be the best for you. However, few can argue that case management is the bulk of what any serious group will do.

What does case management mean? In my opinion, it means the following: initial client contact, investigative design, and data management. Case management fields phone calls, answers emails, and conducts client interviews. The case managers(s) will often initially know more about the case than anyone until an investigation takes place. In this regard, they are often the best ones to determine the size and structure of an investigation, depending on their level of experience.

The first part is the initial client contact, of which are two types. The first are well-known locations that you approach. In most cases, it isn't necessary to conduct initial interviews or historical research. Places like Waverly Hills, Eastern State, the USS Carolina and others have information online. Even local, lesser known sites have enough information posted that the initial interview can be bypassed, for the most part. Honestly, most location managers of oft-investigated sites will not have time to go through all of this with you, in any case.

However, if you are doing an undiscovered site or a residential case, you need to have a preinvestigation plan of action. If your team is new, you may have to be ready to load up the car for ANY case that comes your way. The more experienced and busy you become, the less likely you will be willing to drive sixty miles to investigate a location that basic interviews will reveal to be something nonparanormal.

Here is a breakdown of basic case management:

- Do an email exchange, try to get a good sense of activity. Ask the client to compile a journal of past occurrences and suggest he or she start keeping a journal of events noting dates, times, and any particular emotional events that may be going on at the time to the best of his or her ability. In some cases you can determine nonparanormal explanations from these exchanges alone (your client, however, may not always want to hear that, or he or she may be relieved). The email exchange also gives you a sense of a client's emotional well-being. Of course, you may need to schedule a phone interview at this time to get a better sense of the situation.

- If the location appears to have possible activity, a little bit of historical research is now in order. A homeowner may complain of seeing Civil War apparitions, for example. A quick Internet research may reveal that there were skirmishes in the area, even if no known battles were fought. A quick Internet search can also give you basic property information, for example. One you have previous owner names, if applicable, you can learn a bit about that. Some groups only do superficial research, while others are very extensive. The amount of research you conduct depends on how much time you have to dedicate, and how oriented you are toward research itself. I will advise that it is important to do as much historical research on residential cases as possible; you owe it to the client. Some groups seem to be out every weekend. I imagine that is a fun and exciting way to spend Saturday nights. The reality is that teams who put in a lot of historical research normally cannot do more than one or two investigations a month. It takes time to research a location's history. It also takes time to review evidence. Again, your case load depends on your objectives.

- Schedule and conduct an investigation. This is not as cut and dried as it sounds. One team member has to determine the investigation's objective (debunk, interview more witnesses, document claims). I separate these because the interview process can take a long time. Also, you may focus entirely on debunking and may not get around to doing other types of investigative work, like EVP, for example, during that initial investigation.

- Review and analyze evidence. This stage is time-consuming and not as simple as finding a spectacular instance of EVP. You have to cross check to make sure the EVP isn't contamination, and that any evidence you obtain is not explainable by other means. Ideally, evidence needs to be discussed among the team to determine its legitimacy. This is a LONG process.

- Determine findings (or lack thereof), and compile a report and date for your team and the client. Provide suggestions and recommendations based on the situation. Also determine how evidence will be archived.

- Schedule follow-up with the client to share findings. It doesn't always have to be face-to-face like we see on TV, though it can be if you have uncovered something spectacular or if you have numerous things to share.

- Determine with the client if a follow-up investigation or other services are needed. At this point, you can decide if the case should be closed.

There are many case management models; this was just an example. You will have to find what works best for your team.

History Matters

Paranormal investigation is about many things, but it is especially about engaging history. Investigators are permitting the dead—and history—to speak. Serious teams know how to do serious inquiry into the past. I believe the best moments are when teams uncover previously unknown information about a site. Even more profound is when teams capture evidence that reinforces a site's history. Uncovering new information is often a matter of asking a new set of questions regarding a location's past. Paranormal investigation is not always about the evidence; sometimes it is very much about rediscovering history.

Different types of cases require different modes of inquiry; public historical sites often have existing historical documentation but not always. Various staff or resident historians may promote alternative versions of events or place emphasis on different facts. Any location will have multiple histories to consider. Take a southern planation, for example, or an Indian schoolhouse in the midwest. The dominant history of the white people will not be the same as the slave or Native American narrative.

I was on a case out in rural South Carolina where neighbors in a rural area all reported someone knocking on their doors at strange times in the night. They would open the door to find no one there. One family lived on one ten-acre parcel in this area and claimed to have witnessed Civil War-era apparitions in the woods behind their home. During the investigation, we left a digital audio out in the woods and captured what sounded like musket fire and someone saying, "Get up the hill," along with what sounded like troop movement. That area is known to have experienced skirmishes during the war.

I wanted to suggest to the homeowners to take a metal detector out in the woods and see if they could find any musket balls. Even better, maybe someone could contact a historian in the area or an area university in an effort to obtain more specific military history. How awesome would it be to use evidence collected during investigations to actually influence academic historical inquiry?

Residential cases are often the ones where you have to dig the hardest to find evidence to relate back to your own research. Based on my observations, it seems most teams do only superficial historical research. In-depth inquiry—which is often required to really dig up the goods—is very time-consuming, and most investigators may not know how to do it. I've come across books that suggest investigators should "just go to the courthouse." Yes, you may indeed have to do that, but there are ways to obtain information before you trot downtown.

Online Resources

The Internet has changed the way we understand the paranormal, and also community dynamics. Likewise, it has changed how historical research is conducted. Online resources are now the most easily accessible, but there are emerging ethical issues to consider when researching locations—or clients.

It takes a matter of seconds to pull up basic information on an individual or a location. I want to first touch on researching a client. Many serious teams are a bit selective about where they go. As mentioned earlier, it is not unheard of to do a background check on clients to ensure that a team is not entering a potentially dangerous situation. These things were not a huge issue a decade ago before it become cool to be haunted. However, so many people now report paranormal activity that the safety of your team is a real concern.

We've even considered developing a "code word" to be used to alert other team members if we are ever in a crisis. For example, it was suggested to say the exact phrase "Everything is alright" if we were in a compromising situation in a client's home.

I am not a historical researcher, but I am lucky to have several experienced researchers in my area. During a public event at Körner's Folly in the summer of 2011, one local historian pointed out that the first and most valuable resources are always direct interviews with your client, be it a homeowner or a historic location director. Docents, volunteers, and staff of historical locations often know more that what any book can tell you. Granted, many sites that are consistently investigated do not have time to have the same interview with every team. Sites like Waverly Hills, the USS Carolina, and others will have sufficient information online.

There are moments when even well-known sites demand new lines of historical questioning, and paranormal investigators can first pose these questions to staff. Waverly Hills is an awesome location to investigate and seems to be consistently active. Yet paranormal researchers have uncovered that some commonly held beliefs about the location floating around in the community, such as the high numbers of deaths on site, are not historically accurate. This does not deflect from the site's intriguing history or paranormal claims, however. It just reminds us to be careful about which stories we hold as truths.

Historical Research on Sites and Buildings

There are a few types of historical investigation. The first is "personal histories" based on what staff or site owners know about the location, as well as stories from those who've had paranormal experiences there. Perhaps a client feels that they are seeing a small child roam around the property and a story emerges that a small child died on site? A researcher will go back and see if that occurred. In some cases, such stories are proven to be folklore. So, what explains the child's sighting? Alternatively, what if odd events were merely interpreted as a child and that "story" became truth? Client perceptions and personal beliefs of the living associated with a site can often influence how events are experienced. An ideal situation also allows you to interview former tenants although that is sometimes difficult to do.

Another type of inquiry is "documented history," which includes public records such as deeds, newspaper articles, death and birth certificates, and other related items.

A location's address and documented history is a first step, but you'll have to consider the personal histories of former tenants who lived on the site. These names are often well known. Once you have a name, you have to start doing some archival research.

Did I mention this is really time consuming?

You can search county tax records and deeds, as well as census information to learn about former tenants. There are also many free online resources that will assist, such as the National Archives (www .archives.gov), FamilySearch.org, genealogy-quest.com, and colonial-ancestors.com.

Investigators in the southern US may find the Richmond Leesburg courthouse a wonderful asset; they hold port entry documents. Many east coast residents can find information of their ancestors somewhere in those documents.

Research on Residential Cases

Residential cases present unique concerns. The first mode of research normally revolves around who actually owns the property.

It is generally accepted that it is OK to have teams discreetly come to rental properties without owner permission, although some argue otherwise. I advocate for teams not to show up at people's homes with paranormal-themed car magnets and overbearing announcements of their ghostly mission. Some residents may not appreciate it, and it could freak the neighbors out.

In most cases, it is OK for tenants to have people over for dinner or for parties, for example. An investigation is akin to someone having guests for dinner. However, owner permission is *absolutely necessary* if any information and evidence collected at the site is publicly released. Some landlords may not appreciate having their property labeled as haunted!

Once permission has been established, do a property search from a variety of real estate sources. These searches will tell you a great deal about the location such as square footage, property values, date last sold, and general neighborhood demographics. You can also get the parcel number from these sites to do deed research.

I understand some people find it frightening that one can obtain information so readily, but keep in mind that these are public records. Homeowners can do this research too, but most don't know where to start.

Part of any research may involve getting to know as much about your client as legally possible without being ethically invasive. Social networking sites offer a great source of public information if viewable by the general public. It is advised, however, that one does not friend or follow clients on their private social networking sites. One needs to maintain a professional distance in these circumstances.

In some instances, it may be a good idea to conduct basic background checks on clients to make sure your team isn't entering a dangerous situation. Such checks are not necessary unless you have accepted a case and discover emerging red flags. Sites like beenverified.com offer a good database for about $100 a year and you can discontinue service at any time (there are many such sites). This is not a bad investment if you think you will need to run background checks on select clients and new team members. You can use membership dues to help pay for such services.

Finding that ethical line of inquiry is something we need to think about. One investigator spoke during an event about historical research and shared a situation where she had a case involving teenagers. She came across the teens' publicly accessible Facebook pages and discovered there were quite a few things going on in the family possibly relating to the alleged "paranormal" activity. These issues were not revealed during the interview process, but the investigator decided not to share the teens' public ramblings with the parents, who could easily find their children's Facebook pages if they made the effort. This case called for discretion. It is important to know when to draw boundaries, and it is equally important to keep your search to public records.

The investigator also pointed out that though online resources are extremely valuable, they are also problematic. This is particularly true if you are investigating a public location or a known haunted site and use online resources to obtain information. Wikipedia is an awesome resource and contrary to what some may think, teachers do not automatically hate the site. However, you and every other person who can go online has access to Wikipedia, so any information you come across must be considered public knowledge. A team psychic can easily obtain information prior to an investigation and make a "cold reading" suspect.

Let's break this down step-by-step for a residential investigation with advice from Steve Barrell, from Haunted North Carolina. The first thing to do is to find the current deed. You can do this by accessing online resources. Real estate sites are untapped resources. I like trulia.com and zillow.com. The information is all public, and you can immediately glean the date a house was built, how large it is, the size of the plot, as well as the cost and yearly taxes (which gives you an indication of a client's socioeconomic level).

Once you get a parcel number, go to the county website of where this property is located. Most public records are now online. You go to the tax department (in most cases) and either type in the address or the parcel number. Keep in mind that some online systems may ask for an "old parcel number" which may be a different number sequence. Be sure to see if there are two parcel numbers; it will not always be the case but it does happen. You should be able to find the current deed rather easily. You can then scroll through the deed until you find the book number, and use that to go back to the previous owner. You keep going back further and further until you find all previous owners on record. Note all the owners' names.

Once you have names, you may start researching public birth and death records to see who lived in the home and when they died. If there are living recent occupants, you can do Internet searches to learn more about them. In one case, Steve found that a well-known community figure had lived in a home. The man was a public official and did some business out of the basement. No claims related to this but it was an interesting piece of information to know.

Genealogy searches may arise at some point. Ancestry.com is a wonderful site although one has to pay for access. Archive.com is another great historical research for older properties or sites.

You may have to contact the local courthouse or historical society. They will be more than excited to help you out, in most cases. They live for moments like this and may be able to direct you to local archives where you may find an old diary or other obscure information that may totally change your understanding of the phenomena.

Your local library is also a great resource. Your library card may provide you with free online access to many informational databases throughout your library system depending on the agreement they may have with providers. My local library allows users to peruse some of the state university databases.

Area universities may have research programs or professors dedicated to local history. These are untapped resources for certain historic areas or old homesteads. One university in my city has a program where graduate students have extensively researched my local downtown area. Few people know about this, but what a gold mine! Another area university has a program dedicated to cataloging and dating abandoned area graveyards (some are attached to homesteads, slaves, or Revolutionary War events). Many in the paranormal community often forget about resources offered by local university communities. It never hurts to send an email to a local university's history department explaining the nature of your interest while inquiring if any faculty could engage in relevant historical research. If you make your research about history—and not just ghosts—it is surprising how positively people may respond even if they do not share your paranormal enthusiasm.

Back to the nitty-gritty paperwork: once you have tenant names (past and present), an address, or a historical event you want to research, you can search through newspapers articles to see if anyone did anything noteworthy. This is not has hard as it seems: the National Endowment for the Humanities has created a US newspaper directory with publications dating from 1690. It may take some time to find what you are looking for—and hopefully, you will be searching something specific. What a resource!

Historical research is very tedious, and you will often find dead ends. This process can be just as time-consuming as evidence review. I believe that many teams do not do extensive historical research because it takes up time, can be frustrating, and may not always be necessary.

8: Client Interview and Relations

The client interview is one of the most important elements of any investigation, particularly in residential cases involving specific claims. It is the primary mode in which you collect data—the interview itself may turn out to be the most meaningful data you'll get your hands on.

There are some basic, standard questions that most teams ask, covered later in this section. For now, let us consider a few larger issues before we get into the question list.

In the past, clients often contacted a paranormal team after a series of events had occurred. In many cases, a client would call long after events stopped. Furthermore, contacting a team was a last resort and probably a secretive step on their part. The interview was therefore extremely important for documenting case claims and for getting a sense of timeline, witnesses, and the overall general picture. Likewise, people did not often know the terms used to describe what had happened. Their experiences were dictated by whatever words they knew to best describe the situation. For example, they could say things were moving around, that they felt strange, and sometimes that they heard voices.

However, things are very different today. Many people will immediately call a paranormal team at the very onset of any slightly anomalous event. To make matters more complicated, most are familiar with the appropriate terminology and will no longer use their own vocabulary but what they have heard from popular culture. Now an investigator can get case claims that are sometimes very specific and already analyzed by the client. For example, they may get an email that "something negative" is going on in the house because shadow figures are present. Or that objects are being thrown around by a ghost and that "we've left a digital audio recorder out and caught EVP that said 'get out.'"

My point is this: most people today now know how to make case claims sound urgent and legit. People also think they know how to investigate their homes based on what they see on TV. Likewise, there isn't going to be too much objectivity in investigating your own house if you already feel something going on.

In some instances, cases are very urgent and very legit. There is another reality, as well: thanks to TV, it is almost "cool" for people to have a paranormal team in their home. Some people actually *want* to be haunted or need special attention because other parts of their lives are lacking. I'm being completely honest; teams need to be aware that this reality is out there. Here's why: people who want to be haunted or to have ghosts will always have one, no matter what you do or do not find, no matter how many cleansings take place—there is very little you can do for people who desire to be haunted.

Having said that, one may get a case where truly remarkable activity is occurring and clients are frightened or generally curious about the events. You'll still have to ask the right questions to make sure the client's objectives are transparent.

Scientific Paranormal shared what they call an "intake sheet" or client interview. These questions comprise the standard script most established teams use.

Sample Intake Sheet from Scientific Paranormal

Basic Contact Information

Name:

Age:

Occupation:

Marital status:

Phone number:

Email:

Site Information

Address:

Square footage (approx.):

Type of building (home, restaurant, fort, etc.):

Number of residents/employees on site:

Length of time living of home (or length of time owned):

Rent or own:

Date the site was built:

Number and type of pets (if home):

Number of previous owners (to best of knowledge):

Any recent remodeling:

Any building improvement issues (electrical, plumbing, etc):

Health and Psychology:

Any daily or special medications by those who experienced activity:

Any special health or special consideration needs by those who experienced activity:

Has there been a traumatic experience by anyone who
    experienced activity:

Has anyone been having nightmares or not sleeping well:

Are there any strong religious or other beliefs by anyone who
    experienced activity:

Has anyone in the site been interested or experienced activity before:

Has anyone ever died at this location (best guess):

Information About the Experience:

How long has the paranormal activity been going on:

Did anything significant or memorable precede the onset of activity:

Has this paranormal activity been affecting your daily life:

Names and ages of individuals who have experienced the phenomenon:

Is there anyone living or working on the site who has not experienced
    the paranormal activity:

Has anyone been more negatively affected by the activity:

Have you contacted anyone else about this problem:

What solutions, if any, have you attempted to alleviate this problem:

Activity Detail:

Describe the paranormal activity in full detail. Include all experiences,
    mentions of activity, etc. Be as specific and detailed as possible:

Rooms having activity and in what form (audible, physical, visual, etc):

Client Goals:

What are you hoping the outcome will be from an investigation by
    Scientific Paranormal:

———————————————

That last question is an extremely important one as it is necessary to know the client's objectives.

There are other questions one may ask in addition to the standard script to compensate for paranormal reality TV's influence. Here are a few I would recommend in addition to the preceding:

- Does anyone in the family believe he or she has psychic abilities? This may seem like a silly question, but you'd be surprised to find how many clients insist they have some abilities. Furthermore, this helps you link up psi or determine how connected a client may feel to the activity.

- Ask witnesses to describe their initial gut feelings when the activity occurred. That very first emotion and thought is often the purest, most undiluted emotion during an event. What a client feels as it is occurring, or right after, hits before the self-doubt and second-guessing come into the picture.

- Were there any emotional events or unusual stress the client remembers occurring before the activity? It could have occurred mere hours or even days before the event. If yes, ask the client to describe the event. Even a menstrual cycle may turn out to be significant.

- What do you feel is occurring in your home? What or whom do you feel is behind the possible activity? Again, this may give profound insights. A client may say, "I feel that it may be my granddaddy who passed away" or "I think it's a demon." Those insights go a long way in determining what the client perceives to be the issue.

- What paranormal reality TV shows does the client watch, if any, and what are the person's favorite episodes? This question obviously demonstrates how into this general subject area clients may be.

- How many heating/cooling units (HVAC) are in the home. Sometimes, attic HVAC units can cause the house or floor to "vibrate" or cause EMF to spike when kicking on.

- Ask if anyone has recently stopped taking medications. The abrupt cessation of medications, particularly certain antidepressants or antipsychotic medications, is significant.

General Guidelines
for How to Conduct an Interview

Interviews are the most useful way to collect subjective data, and there are certain protocols needed to make the most of the experience. Again, not everyone is going to be a good interviewer. You need someone on your team who is a good listener and who can ask questions without baiting the client.

Here are some of Haunted North Carolina's guidelines:

- When possible, the case manager or designated investigator should interview all witnesses to the activity (i.e., someone with interview experience). Two members should be present during the interview, and the use of a recorder (audio and/or video) is recommended if witnesses will allow.

- Witnesses should be interviewed privately.

- If possible, begin interviews with the principle witness. Let the person tell the story uninterrupted; further questions can be asked afterward.

- Don't ask leading questions such as "Did the noise sound like _____?" Instead ask, "What did the noise sound like to you?"

- Be tactful at all times. Remember, many people are frightened or worried about the phenomena they may be experiencing.

I want to amend this by suggesting that the first initial interview need not take place face-to-face. Realistically, it is often quite hard to travel to someone's home, particularly if the person isn't local. I recommend investing in a Skype or Google Voice number and an application that allows you to record the phone call (with client permission). Doing so lets you avoids having to provide your private number and also keeps you or other teammates from having to go visit a client if the situation turns out to be rather mundane. Skype recording apps are inexpensive and excellent tools for case management. You can save the file and have it as a part of the case file. More teams are using online resources as integral aspects of their case management system.

There are obvious advantages in conducting on-site interviews. Body language can provide extra clues about a client's emotions. The best interviewers are those on your team who may have a day job dealing with people and interpersonal situations, as not everyone has the ability to interpret body language (few of us are professionally trained in interview techniques like, say, an FBI agent). However, many of us understand that a client may cross his or her arms during moments of slight discomfort. Looking away may also indicate a reluctance to share information.

Someone who fidgets may be nervous, in general. Also, what a client says about certain things reveals tons. HNC was on a case once where a client's home was almost like a transient location for various relatives who needed a place to live. She said she was OK, with this and later made a comment that her house was like "Kool-Aid" in its informal, come-and -go nature. There was tension underlying that comment, which was outwardly meant to be humorous. But that little conversation snippet revealed a great deal about her real feelings on the matter as well as the paranormal claims.

In his legend tripping book, Jeff Belanger shares some great interview tips that work great for private home investigators as well. He points out that some witnesses are outgoing and love to talk, while others are more reserved. The outgoing folks will normally do very well with general questions you can whittle down to specifics as the conversations flows. However, others may need very specific questions to help them get started.

It is also helpful to share a little bit about yourself before and during the interview. Doing so humanizes you and helps the witness develop a connection. You can share if you've had a similar experience for example, but be sure not to lead your witness. One general type of question to avoid is to ask people "if they felt scared" when the event occurred. Always ask how an event made the person feel and let him or her provide the adjective.

Some clients or witnesses may not want to open up, no matter how perky or friendly you are. As Jeff writes, "a good interview should feel like a conversation, because it is one."

It is also useful to try to understand a client's belief language, as that gives you a new path into the person's psyche. Perhaps consider asking clients the same questions I asked you earlier in the book about what they believe concerning ghosts and the afterlife.

These elements give you a good idea of claims and a client mindset. Now, you are ready to actually do some fieldwork!

9: Fieldwork

When you go out to investigate, you are doing what is called fieldwork. The real work of the field isn't literally going to the site; it also involves preparatory work like interviews and historical research. Before you gear up, you are already out in the field, in a way.

Wikipedia says fieldwork is the "collection of raw data in natural settings." That is a fairly succinct description and relevant to what paranormal researchers do. We have already reviewed a most essential part of that fieldwork: the interview.

Before we break down a possible investigation and how it is designed, let's go over a few guidelines about what one should and should not do while out in the field.

Investigation Do's and Don'ts

Haunted North Carolina has a list of what is and is not acceptable during fieldwork. Many teams have a similar list:

- Team members must conduct themselves professionally at all times, dress appropriately (e.g., clean, neat, nonreflective, nonrustling clothing, safe and comfortable footwear, no loose or heavy objects), refrain from alcohol and recreational drug use, refrain from smoking on site (smoke in a designated area away from equipment), and be courteous and polite to all.

- Performance-inhibiting prescription drugs must be reported in confidence to a director and/or case manager.

- Questions from law enforcement, media, or curious bystanders should be referred to a director (or designated team member).

- Remain in visual, audible, or radio contact of another team member at all times.

- Do not engage in horseplay or practical jokes.

- Intuitive or sensitive feelings and sensations should be noted in the investigator's log and not discussed before or during the investigation as to avoid bias or suggestibility.

- No member may carry a weapon without direct permission from a director. Violation of this can result in immediate termination of membership.

- No pets are allowed during investigations except for service animals. These animals must be in the care of their handlers at all times.

- Do not attempt to provoke paranormal entities.

- HNC respects individual members' religious beliefs. Individual members may choose to say a prayer of protection before going to a location and a binding prayer upon leaving.

- No trespassing on private property or in specifically prohibited locations.

- Respect the client's wishes at all times. Do not handle objects or enter rooms without permission.

- If an investigator is asked to do something in conflict with investigation protocols, personal morals, ethics, or beliefs, let a director know in private.

- Each investigator is responsible for his or her own personal safety.

Now that you know what not to do, let us look at a few ways to organize fieldwork.

How to Organize an Investigation

You have a location, a case, and a client. How do you organize your time once on-site? We know how they do it on TV but that isn't the real world. On our cases, there aren't commercial breaks, cued-in music, or nicely edited segments. You've got to make the most of your time—and most of it is going to be rather mundane.

Here are a few steps to help you figure out what to do.

Client Introduction—This is where you introduce the client to your teammates. I highly recommend that all teammates arrive at the same time, or at least initially meet somewhere close to the intended location, maybe a nearby restaurant. Ideally, the team member with whom the client has been in contact should be the first in the door once you arrive on site.

Once the client is introduced to the team, a designated person explains to the client what to expect throughout the evening and asks him or her what time the team needs to leave the home. Make sure all arrangements are clear and that you have the client's contact information should he or she leave the premises. Some clients want to stay during an investigation. It is important to honor their wishes, as you are a guest in their home.

Have the client complete all forms at this time if it hasn't been done already. Also make sure to explain what your team can/cannot do. For example, make it clear that you cannot get rid of a ghost or cleanse a site if that's not part of what your team does. Haunted North Carolina explicitly states that we do not do that and makes it clear our objective is to gather data in hopes of possibly helping the client understand what may or may not be occurring.

Site Mapping—This is basically mapping out the location, whether it is hand-drawing a layout of the home or making a map of the land. Site mapping normally takes place with the lights on. This includes pictures of the location and surroundings, as well as any notations about the area. For example, you may see a cell phone tower close by. Note it. Train tracks are in the backyard. That's significant. The home may be close to a military base where the occasional ammunition goes off. That's also significant. Note anything you feel may be significant, even if the neighbors have a pool and there are kids outside swimming in it. You can also use the blueprints to log any activity for your team's case files or as part of the final report you provide to the client

HNC actually draws a blueprint of the property for case files. It doesn't have to be perfect, but it should either be a reasonable blueprint of the building, home, or the larger property. Ideally, this should take place before an investigation but that is not always possible.

I also recommend that establishing photos of the environs be taken at this time (with the lights on). This means you take pictures of rooms, locations, and other significant areas. We'll explore photography in more detail later.

Base Readings—The team case obtain base readings during site mapping. Base readings refer to EMF readings and other environmental anomalies that may be present. This is also where a blueprint is necessary. Many investigators walk around with a K-II meter or EMF gauge. Here is some basic protocol for using it:

- Walk slowly. Sudden movements can cause false readings.

- Keep the device extended away from your body as it can cause the device to spike.

- Note any appliances or areas where EMF is high. The base for most new homes is 0.0 mG–2.0 mG. However, properties with older wiring may be erratic or even off the charts. David Rountree has a very useful technique for mapping EMF in homes that aren't "flat." Walk the room as one would in a search-and-rescue mission, meaning gauging EVP in a grid-like manner throughout the room. I have been in historic sites where this is the only way to get a true, accurate baseline EMF reading when it varied widely between different spots in the room. It is always advisable to do this with the lights on for obvious reasons. However, some older properties have too much EMF noise with the lights, so it is hard to get accurate baseline readings. Körner's Folly is one example—the lights turned on create readings sometimes up to 5.0 mG higher than when off!

- Note temperature and any other environmental data you might be collecting (humidity, etc). Keep in mind that like EMF, these things may need to be monitored throughout the investigation.

Once base readings are done, determine the investigation's structure and teams if this isn't already organized. This is also when you can start setting up equipment if it not already in place.

Client Interview, Again—Ideally, a thorough client interview has already occurred. However, HNC believes that sometimes an on-site interview may actually help activity manifest. This may also be the first face-to-face interview if you've previously spoken over the phone. One can hopefully video record the interview or at least have a digital audio recording. It may also be interesting to note how the client responds to questions in person.

Keep in mind that equipment setup and client interview(s) can take some time, particularly if one is using a digital video recording system and if there are multiple witnesses to interview. Please factor interviews, equipment setup, and breakdown into your total investigative design, and allot plenty of time for everything. Also make sure batteries and equipment are in working order before you arrive at a location, or else time will be wasted taking care of these issues.

Something to Know: Blueprints

Here is one way we use such blueprints: we ask certain investigators to do an initial walkthrough "blind," meaning we send in investigators who have no knowledge about the case claims to go in and mark on their blueprints where they "sense" activity may occur. It does not matter if the investigators are sensitive or not—studies have indicated that skeptics sometimes identify the same areas as psychics as being "creepy" or weird. Investigators do this individually, it isn't a group effort. We then fold these up and revisit them after evidence review to see if there are any correlations. Obviously, the walkthrough needs to take place before the client or case manager discusses client claims with other members on the team.

Investigative Sessions

Most investigations involve teams members breaking into small groups and rotating through a location's hotspots. That's one way to do it and is also the most common depiction of fieldwork seen on TV.

Sessions can involve active debunking, EVP work, or static stations, meaning setting up camera or audio, then leaving the area undisturbed.

They can also be experimental in nature, depending on investigation objectives.

One needs to determine how to design sessions based on the claims. Depending on the situation, you can experiment with both the human element and the static element. David Rountree tends to set up equipment and then observe the environment remotely. There may be instances where remote observation is desirable, particularly if one has the equipment to do so.

Today, most investigators organize their sessions around EVP work, as it is the easiest way to engage the investigative experience and provides what many feel to be the most compelling evidence.

However, the sessions need to be in the same conditions as when the activity is experienced. For example, if activity occurs when children are present and seems to center around them, it may be necessary to investigate with the children there, at least for a short time.

I am not suggesting that children be part of the investigation, nor am I suggesting you turn off the lights and throw a child into the middle of an EVP session. (That's actually ill-advised!) What I am saying is that it is imperative to investigate under the conditions where the claims were experienced.

If a client complains that a ghost shakes things in the dining room during dinner, you should investigate at that time. Obviously, that doesn't mean that you sit around the dinner table asking EVP questions. What it means is that you set up your equipment and observe the family as they are eating.

Once you determine your sessions, figure out the timeframe based on how much time you have at the location. We tend to go in twenty- to thirty-minute sessions in small teams and rotate through the site, but it is always determined by the size of the location, the team, and the case claims.

EVP is the most common way to engage the environment, but there is also some merit in the "vigil"—in sitting still and observing. Another common practice is to use K-II meters and other devices as the medium for interaction. One can also mimic or try to replicate a certain circumstance when activity occurred.

The initial investigation is often just that: an investigation to assess what is going on, focusing on finding alternative explanations, and trying to obtain any evidence. But initial investigations may not yield much in terms of evidence. It is often necessary to return, particularly if the client or location continues to experience activity.

Something to Know: Going Dark

Here is where investigation design gets tricky and contradicts what you see on TV. Real investigation does not necessarily take place in the dark. In fact, Loyd Auerbach and many parapsychologists suggest going dark actually makes it harder to assess activity, particularly if the claims involve moving objects or other phenomena where clarity and transparency are necessary. Most investigators investigate in the dark because that is what they see on TV. Furthermore, many homeowners experience activity at night because that is when they are home, winding down and less distracted by daily habits. Lastly, investigators most often investigate at night because that's when they have time to do it! Philosophically, it isn't necessary to have all the lights out.

Rountree points out that cutting off lights may cut down on EMF noise, and I have been on cases where that is certainly true. Complete darkness makes it fun and creepy, but it isn't an absolute necessity. Low light conditions are ideal for infrared technology like night vision and may be amenable to capturing certain phenomena.

Jim Hall took HNC on the Travel Channel in 2006. HNC was investigating the USS Carolina, where Jim insisted to producers the lights remain on. The lights stayed on, and the results were just as compelling.

That episode is up at the HNC website, so you can see how a lights-on (or daytime) investigation works.

I get it though—most investigations now take place in the dark, or at least at night. Consider whether going dark is always the practical thing to do based on the client's claims.

We have gone over the basics of how to start a group, get cases, and conduct a basic investigation. Now let us look at when things don't go so smoothly.

10: When Things Get Bumpy

There are moments in investigations when you are going to run into difficult people. You may encounter homeowners who expect more than you can provide or don't like what you have to tell them. You may run into unscrupulous managers of historic locations. Most likely, you are going to experience some discomfort with other investigators. These things happen.

Before taking on a residential case, here are a few questions to ask yourself and your teammates. In fact, it is good to include this in official protocol:

- How will I (or my team) handle the situation if we do not find evidence to back up a client's claims and he/she becomes angry?

- What if the team finds evidence (historically or otherwise) of something potentially disturbing? How do we approach the client about that?

- What if the client does not like our findings and decides to publicly discredit us?

- Are we able, as a team, to provide the client with a list of outside resources such as clergy, psychologists, and other experts if we feel such services are needed?

- Are we able to legally discern what we can/not say to individuals about their emotional and mental conditions?

- How do we deal with a client bringing in multiple teams and comparing what we find to other collected evidence?

- What if the client (or investigator) becomes distressed and/or confrontational during an investigation?

- How do we handle a case where a client just wants to "show off" that he/she has paranormal investigators in the house?

- What is our procedure if we encounter illegal drug use or child abuse during the investigation, particularly if the client has indicated this is a confidential case?

The Unseen Troublemakers

There are times when you may encounter things on investigation that make you uncomfortable—and this does not include the living.

I was once with a reverend observing a house blessing for a client who felt there was possibly something negative in the home. Our investigation yielded no evidence of anything at all but the client requested a blessing. As a group, HNC does not do that, but we will refer clients to clergy who can provide this service free of charge. I came along to observe. Those present at the blessing were the reverend, the client, her mother, and myself.

The blessing and cleansing involved reading scripture and praying at various locations in the home. The reverend had salt, holy water, and blessed oil. She blessed and sealed every opening in the home, leaving a symbolic pathway for the spirit to leave the home at any point.

The next-to-last stop was the attic bedroom. This pathway was the last closed. As the reverend moved to bless the window over the bed, all four of us in the room heard an audible growl that seemed to come from the air in front of the reverend. She stopped.

"Did you all just hear that?" she asked.

All four of us had indeed heard the feral, animal-type growl. It was almost unbelievable because there were no malicious feelings, horrible odors, or anything one would associate with such a growl.

The revered asked the growler to leave this location in the name of Jesus Christ. Everyone remained calm. There were no more growls heard during the cleansing. The client, however, claimed the activity continued. The reverend returned to perform another blessing and cleansing, and also recommended a symbolic memorial service to help lay whatever may have been there to rest. Despite the growl, neither HNC nor the reverend assumed this case to be demonic.

It is hard to assess what occurred on this particular case, as the client seemed uninterested in having the team back for a longer investigation or the memorial service. There was no time during our investigations or cleansings that anyone felt threatened, "off," or oppressed by negative energy. We surmised whether the client herself was the agent, though maybe subconsciously. But of course, I know I heard that growl.

There may be times when one encounters things that just defy explanation. While these things may not be evil or dark, many investigators feel they have to be spiritually protected during cases. Many investigators privately say a protection prayer before an investigation, others do it as a group. How you go about it depends on you and your group's overall philosophy. I have heard that Patti Star, a Kentucky-based investigator and Scarefest organizer, always starts off her investigation saying, "Sweet spirits, please come talk to us." What a lovely way to open an EVP session.

Remember, there are cases that aren't always so sweet. Let me be clear in suggesting that negative cases may not always be demonic. There is evidence suggesting that our own subconscious can unleash mighty forces when the conditions are right. I do acknowledge that the world of the unseen is more complex than many realize and some feel the need to manage these more esoteric elements.

Michelle Belanger has written extensively on psychic protection. She is a personal friend and one of the most intelligent people I have ever encountered. She provides great advice when it comes to being open to all considerations (demonic and otherwise) during investigation. She says, "When a team is dedicated purely to discovering the truth about paranormal phenomena, it has the luxury of many different belief systems."

With that in mind, let us move into what to do if you find yourself in an oppressive investigative environment.

You may enter a location and immediately feel uncomfortable. The first thing to do is to rule out high EMF or other natural things that may physically affect you. If you do feel uncomfortable—you may experience heaviness, a headache, or even nausea—you need to ground yourself.

Grounding yourself can be done in one of many ways. Belanger recommends visualizing negative energy literally leaving your body and being replaced by positive energy. She suggests you stand on the ground with feet apart, take three deep cleansing breaths, and visualize the bad energy leaving. Reverse that visualization to include positive energy entering your body to displace what has left.

This sounds "woo-woo" for some, but I think these exercises are also useful mental preparation for any investigation regardless if one believes in negative entities. Such exercises help get you in a clear mindset for an investigation and perhaps make you more open to experiencing and receiving paranormal phenomena.

Some feel it is necessary to shield during investigation as a form of protection, which is like visualizing some type of psychic barrier between you and whatever negativity may be present. However, there are investigators who feel that shielding somehow inhibits the ability to sense things. I tend to agree with this statement, although I am not a particularly heightened sensor—the shielding makes me feel claustrophobic. I want to feel the environment's energy. Again, the decision is personal.

Many investigators close with a prayer or statement suggesting that whatever is there is not allowed to follow them home. Again, this is a matter of personal opinion, and everyone must acknowledge whatever he or she feels to be the truth.

It does appear that the majority of today's ghost hunters are influenced by TV and are less familiar with esoteric, magickal elements of the paranormal as opposed to the "scientific" approach. When you start discussing prayers of protection and cleansings, the scientific approach is displaced in favor of the spiritual.

I know plenty of energy workers and clergy who feel called to cleanse, bless, and bind spirits—and they do a good job of it within their own spiritual philosophies. This suggests that elements or energies in existence respond to intent more than they do to one particular faith system, which is a great lesson for clients. Energy workers have to make sure that they really want the entity to leave, because I believe a client can almost "bind" an entity to the location if there is any intent to not let it go. Likewise, a client verbally asserting that ghosts or spirits are unwelcome may do wonders for activity to cease. As Michelle writes, "It's surprising how many people will endure a haunting without ever trying to communicate with the thing that is haunting them. And yet this would solve a great many hauntings."

One important thing I'll state is that no investigator should ever make claims that cannot be ethically backed up. For example, it is unreasonable to tell a client he or she has a demonic entity in the house when there is little evidence suggesting so. Keep in mind that there are divergent views on the demon issue in the community. One has to be very careful in dealing with such claims.

I knew of a case once that involved parent who claimed her autistic child was being demonically attacked. There were no signs of anything negative at all. Somehow, a psychic from outside the team got involved (she had some loose connection but was not speaking on the team's behalf) and made some of the most ridiculous claims. She never visited the site or the client but consulted over the phone that not only were there demons, but also monsters, fairies, and perhaps even haunted dust bunnies in the home. In order to get rid of all of these things, the client had to undergo some extensive magic ritual that seemed so complex even quantum physicists couldn't make sense of it. The client was freaking out and unsure of what to do as her world had just gotten really, really complicated. In the end, the autistic child was just a toddler having very normal temper tantrums perhaps made a bit more complicated by the autism. Second, we suspected that the child might have developed autism-related seizures. We recommended not one, but perhaps two medical opinions on the matter. Regardless, there were no demons or malevolent dust bunnies.

This incident demonstrates that there are fine invisible lines—and some very obvious ones—that investigators need not cross in labeling any case as negative or demonic. The best teams will always advise a client to seek out medical advice or counseling. Loyd Auerbach is leading a national effort to have a list of paranormal-friendly psychologists who can help people who are dealing with what they feel to be paranormal events. He has found that transpersonal psychologists seem to be open to these issues more so than traditional therapists.

Some investigators will encounter truly odd situations on investigation that demand thinking beyond a client's medical and emotional states. I asked Reverend James to clue me in on what to look for in potentially demonic cases. She pointed out that "no two demonic cases will ever be the same. Though similarities may exist, it is important to realize that anyone dealing with the negative must be flexible and open to adjusting their techniques and their customs based on the client's needs and depending on the actions of a demon or negative entity." Rev. James said that as a Christian minister, she will always deal with the demonic in the name of Jesus. However, the prayers and techniques she uses varies depending on the demon's actions and what takes place at the location.

Other investigators have echoed this sentiment too. Rev. James continues:

> One of the greatest skills of demons is to mess with people by making clients and investigators wonder if what is happening is real. Demons may cause obvious manifestations, but sometimes they will simply hide to cause disharmony and questioning. Thus it may be difficult for investigators or exorcists to discover a demon or a negative entity, especially if it is not ready to do battle or it realizes that a team or exorcist may actually be able to bind it and/or to drive it away. When the team leaves, the demon may then re-emerge and the clients may be even more distraught. Trained teams need to be aware of this demonic strategy and forewarn their clients that they may need to come back more than once to a location.

John Zaffis, Keith Johnson, and Reverend James stress that dealing with the demonic or the negative should never to be taken lightly or to be treated as a game. When it comes to negative cases, in my faith belief system, every paranormal team member, demonologist, or exorcist, should be called by his or her deity to deal with the demonic and negative entities as a part of his or her individual ministry.

In James's opinion, attempting to deal with a demonic case without the backing of your Lord is like trying to play with a cobra. "For the sake of the investigators and the client," she stresses, "I sincerely hope that all teams will call in trained professional—before attempting to deal with negative cases on their own."

There are more investigators who claim to perform exorcisms. I have no experience with this and prefer to leave this discussion up to those more qualified. But I want to get back to ethics. I have seen normal paranormal teams go in and film exorcisms—or what they claimed to be as such—and promptly put it online. This is problematic: it exposes the client to social ridicule and professional liability, and suggests the team is more sensationalistic than professional in their approach.

....

Something to Know: Got a Demon?

Some believe there are tangible signs of negative, demonic hauntings. This topic is open for debate, but here is one list of what some believe are strong indicators of such cases:

- Mental instability of a client, high stress levels, and possible drug, alcohol abuse

- Large moving objects

- Unusual sounds such as banging or growling

- An overbearing feeling of heaviness or oppression

- Unexplained scratches or bruises, physical attacks

- Pets acting strangely, afraid, or agitated for no reason

These are very vague signs that may also point to a host of non-demonic issues, including traditional PK-type cases. Likewise, the presence of depression and stress do not automatically translate into demonic oppression! Always be mindful of how you label a case.

....

11: Understanding Evidence

Spotlight: Electronic Voice Phenomena

In 2009, I took a survey of 172 paranormal investigators from the US and Canada. Most suggested that the strongest form of paranormal evidence is Electronic Voice Phenomena, EVP for short.

Electronic Voice Phenomena are voices captured on recording devices that have no known *physical* source. EVP normally relates to voices and not sounds such as phantom footsteps, which are a type of audio anomaly considered to be different than EVP.

Notice that I say "EVP" and not "EVPs." There is a reason for this: the term "EVPs" is grammatically incorrect, despite how often we hear it on TV. EVP can be singular or plural. Electronic Voice *Phenomenon* is singular while the word *phenomena* is plural. I bring it up because so many of us claim to be scientific, yet scientists pick up on such grammatical oversights. The use of "EVPs" makes the community appear misinformed to outsiders. Yes, I know it's annoying to interrupt the flow with a grammar lesson, but now you know.

Video and photographic evidence is almost always problematic and subject to intense scrutiny. It is rare that one gets such crisp, clear video or pictures of something truly anomalous. EVP is fascinating and distinctive for a few reasons. First, it seems to be some of the easiest evidence to obtain. However, it is very rare to recover more than a few strong EVP (if at all) from any investigation. Some EVP appear to be interactive and aware of our presence. This type of evidence is tantalizing and exciting, regardless of how EVP works.

EVP data has great appeal because we find direct information upon evidence review—voices that may answer a specific question or even comment on what an investigator is wearing. These "voices" are even more compelling when one can demonstrate the source was not another investigator or an environmental factor.

There are few things as exciting as recovering an EVP from an investigation. In a way, hearing a recorded voice gives us a personal connection to the activity. The first EVP I ever captured was a direct-response one, meaning that it answered a question. The event centered on an investigator's pink purse. We noticed a huge EMF surge around her purse and could not identify any source (it was lying on a bed). I asked, "Do you like that pink purse?" Upon review, I heard a voice of a young woman with a thick southern accent reply, "Yes." My recorder was the only one that captured the EVP, therefore suggesting that the voice did not belong to the other two female investigators with me at the time. Obtaining this type of evidence creates actual data as well as a powerful personal experience. It is little wonder many investigators find EVP so compelling.

EVP is controversial even among those who research the paranormal. There is no consensus on how EVP works, the best way to capture it, or how it ends up on a recording device. After all, the "talking" is coming from something that does not have a physical body, meaning there is no voice box to push air through, therefore there is nothing to create the waves that filter into our ears to become "sound." Some investigators insist that EVP is not sound at all because the physical mechanisms needed to create these auditory frequencies are absent.

A Brief History of EVP Research

Trying to record ghosts or the departed goes back quite a ways, and like most great discoveries, came about by accident. EVP work is interesting because it really shows how technology influences and changes what we understand and believe about ghosts and hauntings.

Jeff Belanger writes that the first potential spirit voice on "tape" occurred in 1901 when American ethnologist Waldemar Bogoras recorded a spirit conjuring ritual among the Tchouktchi tribe. Apparently, Russian and English speaking voices emerged on the recordings, despite it being only him and the shaman in the room, who didn't speak Russian. Bogoras didn't know he captured EVP; he wasn't thinking along those lines.

It is widely believed that Swedish painter and film producer Friedrich Jürgenson accidentally recorded EVP in 1957. Unlike Bogoras, he knew he'd captured something ethereal.

Jürgenson was recording birds and captured something he initially thought to be stray radio broadcast waves. Jürgenson went on to record thousands of EVP. He also worked with Konstantin Raudive, another seminal figure in EVP research. Contemporary researcher and author Konstantinos has written wonderful works on EVP and spirit communication from scientific and esoteric perspectives, providing a thorough account of EVP research.

EVP is a vast field in itself with regards to research, and it is well worth seeking out books dedicated exclusively to EVP work.

Hailing from the United Kingdom, Raymond Cass was another EVP pioneer. Many do not know about him, but he was significant because he recorded EVP in polyglot form, meaning he claimed to have captured EVP of voices speaking different languages at the same time.

Here in the States, Sarah Estep founded the Association of Trans-communication in 1982. Back then it was called the American Association of Electronic Voice Phenomena. Tom and Lisa Butler took the helm in 2000. The organization's name changed to ATransC to reflect the organization's growing scientific and technical orientation. The Butlers served as consultants for the Michael Keaton 2005 movie *White Noise*, which helped popularize EVP work in conjunction with reality TV. Most importantly, the ATransC has made significant gains in establishing protocol and controlled EVP study.

No on knows why we get these voices on our recorders but there are some opinions out there regarding possible sources. Following is a similar list compiled by the ATransC:

- *Radio Frequency Interference (RFT)*—The explanation that we are merely picking up radio waves is a favorite source for those skeptical of EVP. However, many point out that RFT does not answer specific questions. It is highly unlikely that RFT will be so detailed as to address something that may be occurring during the investigation at the time. Researcher Alexander McCrea conducted EVP research inside a Faraday cage, a device specially designed to keep out all stray radio, microwave, and other waves. He obtained one EVP during his experiment, and this sample was subjected to human voice analysis that concluded the EVP came from no natural source.

It is certainly possible that some EVP are indeed random radio or broadcast waves, for surely our environment is bombarded with these. Yet, McCrea's work demonstrates that there is some sort of unknown process that results in EVP. You can certainly attempt to put your digital audio device in a microwave during EVP sessions at a haunted location. Small microwaves are heavily shielded, meaning they provide a barrier between random radio waves in the environment. Please do not turn the microwave on, however.

- *Experimenter Effect*—This is the assumption that some investigators have the ability to psychically (and subconsciously) imprint responses on recording devices. Psi plays a role here. Many teams notice there are certain investigators who consistently obtain more solid EVP than others. One assumption is that these people are more sensitive and entities are just drawn to them. Parapsychologists assert that individuals with psychic abilities may indeed capture more EVP...because they are subconsciously creating it.

There are studies where EVP has been captured from sleeping subjects. These took place in a controlled environment and yielded that EVP can apparently transmit from people during their nocturnal bliss. HNC once captured an EVP that suggests there may be something to this hypothesis. We do have a sensitive person on our team who was at an investigation. You hear him talking in the background, but then you also hear a voice that sounds just like his speaking over him in EVP fashion! I am not suggesting that the experimenter effect causes all EVP, but it is certainly something to consider. EVP is no less impressive than if ghosts or spirits are speaking to us. In fact, this is compelling evidence that consciousness exists and can be projected into an environment.

- *Interdimensional Beings and Aliens*—There is an idea that we aren't necessarily communicating with ghosts, but with demons, djinn, or aliens. This idea does not resonate with contemporary ghost hunters, but it is present as a possible hypothesis. Some ITC researchers feel they have communicated with interdimensional beings during such sessions. Rosemary Ellen Guiley has ITC captured evidence she feels are from djinn. There may not be too much focus on this particularly hypothesis, but it is certainly something to consider depending on the case claims.

Perhaps embedded in this perspective is the possibility that some EVP are literal time slips, meaning that we aren't catching something dead, but we may be capturing the response of someone living in the 1800s reacting to an apparition of weird-looking people in jeans and black T-shirts vibrating in the kitchen corner.

- *Disembodied Energies*—This is the premise most investigators work with: we are communicating with spirits or ghosts. It is extremely difficult to prove if this is the case. However, what is fascinating is when EVP sessions obtain evidence that is often so specific and can be proven historically. These cases suggest that some form of disincarnate intelligence is the source.

- *Place Memory/Residual*—These are residual sounds or utterances that remain in the environment. Some apparitions appear to be residual, and some phantom sounds may be like footsteps or cannon fire as well. Some EVP are nonsensical phrases or out-of-context words for whatever is occurring at the time. It is hard to know the cause of these sonic imprints. It appears that residual sounds can sometimes be heard audibly and are therefore not actually EVP but a different type of phenomena.

- *Pareidoila*—Pareidoila is a big word with a simple meaning: it is the psychological act of turning an event, namely audio or visual, into something with significant meaning. Let me translate: this is the act of investigators assigning paranormal meaning to otherwise normal environmental sounds (or pictures) that may have gone unnoticed at the time. This is perhaps the largest source of false positive EVP, as a large number of investigators easily mistake nonparanormal sounds as EVP. Another way of describing pareidoila is like "matrixing" where our ears (and eyes) will inherently seek out patterns in what we see or hear in efforts make sense of the information.

Studies have shown that listeners will interpret benign sounds as words during EVP listening exercises. Dr. Mark Leary conducted such a study containing some valid EVP captured at one haunted location. He threw in two nonspirit sounds as well: the sounds of him writing on a chalkboard, for example. Some listeners assigned words to these audio artifacts, interpreting them as real EVP!

Interestingly, the study also noted that most listeners did not detect "emotion" even in legit EVP, meaning there were few who considered a voice to be sad, happy, or angry, etc. Dr. Leary pointed out that those who did interpret emotion from the EVP related it back to their own personality types (he conducted a personality study of those who participated).

We are designed to find patterns in objects and sounds, so it comes as no surprise that we have a tendency to interpret mundane audio data as significant. There is almost a "need" to do so. It is also no surprise that our EVP interpretation is based on our own world views and personalities. I hate to say this, but some people are going to hear what they want to hear when it comes to EVP. With this in mind, it is imperative that investigators take care when assessing all collected evidence, EVP or otherwise.

Further EVP Considerations

What is EVP? How does it work?

These are questions that everyone asks but few can reach a consensus on. EVP is generally thought of as "a voice that shouldn't be there." In truth, what we generally dub as EVP is probably a collection of different phenomena.

ATransC postulates that an entity may use the audio vibrations present in the environment to modulate into a type of speech that ends up on our recorders. This hypothesis holds that a white noise source such as a fan or running water aids the collection of EVP as it supplies ambient noise an entity may use to form words.

Others believe that EVP is tied to electromagnetic fields (EMF) and is therefore not an audio phenomenon at all. David Rountree explains this hypothesis in his book *Paranormal Technology*. He noticed in his study that EVP is almost always associated with EMF fluctuations. He has developed devices that can capture EVP and monitor EMF and has discovered surprising correlations suggesting that EMF plays some variable role in EVP.

Loyd Auerbach has indicated that ghosts use psi to communicate, meaning EVP is partly related to telepathy. He uses one example of how a spirit imprinted messages on blank cassette tapes that were left out overnight. The cassette tapes were just removed from their wrappers and had a magnet waved over them to erase any chance of data. Yet voices did indeed appeared on the tapes. Makes you go hmm, right?

So what does this mean?

The hypothesized mechanisms of EVP determine what may be the best way to obtain audio evidence. David Rountree recommends an external dynamic microphone for a digital audio recorder as essential. Such devices are reasonably priced at stores such as Radio Shack. Rountree theorizes these microphones are useful because the inside coil serves as an EVP conductor. Troy Taylor also recommends using an external microphone placed several feet from the recorder to avoid a hum or buzz.

White noise is considered an aid but EVP are often captured without the use of any ambient enhancers. It is worth experimenting with white noise such as running fans or a faucet to see if you obtain better results. Rountree, however, feels this is unnecessary and counterproductive.

One common complaint is about why EVP is most often obtained in English (place memory being the exception). This question is often related to EVP captured on shows such as SyFy's *Ghost Hunters International,* where investigators are often depicted asking questions in English—and sometimes getting EVP back in English. I know the cast does try to learn phrases in local languages and will try to incorporate it in EVP work.

However, cast members don't always have time to become conversant in foreign languages, and it may not be necessary in the first place.

Alexander McRae has conducted research in areas where no English language radio or TV exists, yet he obtained EVP in English. This leads to the hypotheses that EVP will most often occur in the investigator's language, suggesting a strong psi component. It is possible the experimenter effect is at play, or entities present are telepathically able to communicate in a way that is "translated" into a language the investigator will recognize. More esoteric, eclectic philosophies suggest that once a soul is no longer bound to physical body, they are able to tap into a collective consciousness that transcends language.

It appears that asking questions out loud in whatever language you prefer generates more EVP than silently (or psychically) asking questions. This is not a blanket statement, however, as many investigators have captured responses *just prior* to a question being asked. Again, this suggests that any intelligent entity is capable of telepathy and that we are capable of producing EVP phenomena ourselves.

We had one investigation where EVP of a child was clearly heard upon playback. The EVP commented on a child's table being used for equipment. An etheric small utterance said, "Spider Man table!" with full EVP characteristics. The audio has a little child voice making the statement seconds before a living investigator seemingly mimicked the spirit voice. Weird, right? Was this telepathy between the living and the dead, or the living somehow subconsciously projecting the EVP? Right now, we have no way of assessing what is really going on, but we do have evidence that something unexplained is going on indeed.

It is essential to understand the role *we* play in collecting EVP. ATransC discovered that a "newness" effect also seems to increase the amount of EVP captured. This "newness" is related to the enthusiasm of a new investigator or device out in the field. This brings up the role of intent, which is a variable proven to be statistically significant in positive results during psychical research (such as ESP, telepathy, and remote viewing). I discussed earlier in the book how quantum physicists understand the role of the observer (intent). There may be something to this. John McMoneagle, Stargate's remote viewer, openly said that intent seemed to make a huge difference his own military-intelligence-related remote viewing experiments.

Finally, well-designed studies suggest that some investigators are more attuned to hearing EVP than others—literally. EVP is akin to trying to understand a new language. There are some individuals who cannot decipher a Class A EVP, while others may reach a consensus on what is being said. Gender considerations are also taken into account: women seem to reach consensus more often than men on what is being said. It may be that women have a biological advantage as females can hear a slightly larger portion of audio frequency spectrum.

EVP often falls into frequencies below human speech, but there are many exceptions too. Likewise, ATransC site EVP may often be present on only one recorder during an investigation, but I have found EVP collected on more than one recorder present but not every recorder in the room.

It is important note that traditional wisdom in the past stipulated that the cheaper, lower-end digital recording models were somehow better able to capture EVP. There is now a move away from that logic because of too many false positives associated with ambiguous sounds from lower-end models. More investigators are investing in semiprofessional digital audio recorders, which are comparable in cost to lower-end models. Spending a little extra money may be a wise investment. As one investigator put it, "At least you know when it is a cricket chirping." Lower-end models, he pointed out, have sometimes caused that same sound to come off like a muffled childlike laughter.

You can see that seasoned investigators have not reached a consensus on what EVP is, how it works, or the best way to collect it. Despite the debates, there are a few standard practices deemed useful for successful EVP research.

Best Practices for EVP Work

- Use a digital audio recorder. Record in .wav file format and at the highest sampling rate possible.

- Verbalize EVP questions with 15–30 second pauses in between. Perhaps repeat the question more than once.

- Tag all unusual sounds in the environment so they are not later interpreted as anomalous.

- Occasionally verbally time-stamp the session for reference. This is helpful even if you have a digital time stamp on the recorder. Try to synchronize the clocks on all audio and video equipment at the start of the investigation so everyone is on the same page, timewise.

- Ideally, all investigators present should be in view of a camera in order to eliminate an investigator being a source.

- Have a control recorder, or at least more than one recorder running during all EVP work.

- When saving EVP, collectively decide on a standardized file-naming format used by everyone in your group.

- When clipping EVP samples, develop protocol. For example, don't merely clip the EVP itself; allow for at least 10 seconds before and after so a listener understands the context. In some cases, it you may need to allow for more context in the clip, depending on the EVP captured.

....

Something to Know: Cool Tips!

- Experiment with dynamic external microphones to see what produces better results for you

- Experiment with different genders and modes of questioning

- Try various different audio devices and see what obtains the best evidence

- Experiment with white noise

- Try the standard EVP question session, then do another informal, chit-chat style session among investigators; some of the best EVP is captured during normal conversation

....

Instrumental Trans Communication (ITC) Research

Investigators today are intrigued by the possibility of any sort of spirit communication. Again, there is a history to talking with the dead. Many are familiar with the belief that Thomas Edison was intrigued by the possibility and dedicated some research to the cause. ATransC's research suggests that Edison was less interested than history has led us to believe. Their website said Edison did say he researched "telephoning the dead," yet later admitted making it up. Whatever version is true, the emergence of audio technology has altered the way we conduct investigation as well as what we understand about the spirit world.

Jeff Belanger sums up ITC as "the process of using technology to make contact with the spirit world." ITC can be as simple as asking a spirit to light up the K-II device or as complex as using custom-made spirit and ghost boxes that claim to communicate with the departed in real time.

There are devices specifically created or altered for paranormal research that scan radio frequencies at a super fast speed. It is hypothesized that spirits can manipulate the waves and speak in real time. There are other ITC devices, such as the ovilus and puck, which operate differently but promise the same result: real-time communication with the departed. This equipment is highly controversial in the research community, and any evidence collected on these devices should be carefully scrutinized. This does not mean, however, that one cannot experiment with ITCs on investigation. For now, experimentation is the operative word.

ITC work does not refer only to technology regarding sound or video alone. Flashlights have become a favorite ITC experimental tool for many, despite the technique being controversial and potentially scientifically unsound. The standard way is to use a basic flashlight as ITC is to use one with a button on the end. Unscrew the back just enough that the button can be pushed with only the slightest of touches. (Some even suggest you clip the spring in the back, but that may be problematic). Set the flashlight down and observe it to make sure that it isn't going to go on and off by itself. This may happen, as the spring may expand and contract if the temperature changes. Once the flashlight appears stable, you can then ask a spirit to use it to communicate by turning lights on or off. If by chance you start to get a response (and this does not happen very often), ask an entity to turn the flashlight on for a "yes." Switch instructions to see if it follows suit.

HNC was on a case where we had convincing ITC interaction with a flashlight for a good minute or so. It dimmed the light when we asked, it turned it off when we asked, it made the light brighter when we asked. Britt Griffith of *Ghost Hunters* mentioned in a lecture that he once set up different colored flashlights in a row and specified the spirit to turn on a specific color flashlight—with success. This happened during a public event and the flashlights belonged to the participants. That sort of thing is, well, cool!

ITC work can be used with any technology and is most useful if it is filmed and documented. The most accessible ITC devices for investigators are EMF meters, TriField meters, geophones, or any handheld option that can be used for direct interaction. Keep in mind that you must rule out numerous other variables during any type of ITC work to make sure that you are getting a direct response. Furthermore, having a flashlight or EMF meter spike once or twice doesn't really mean much. Always try to film these events then go through the video second by second to observe any environmental anomalies that may affect whatever device is being used.

Here is one way to put things into perspective. Say you are getting direct response from a flashlight or EMF device. Afterwards, add up the responses you get out of the total numbers asked and try to derive a percentage. You may be really excited about a few responses only to find that you obtained direct response to only 20 percent of the questions asked. I admit that I do not know the "magical" threshold percentage that will make something truly paranormal. But I will suggest that anything above the 50-percent mark needs to be carefully interpreted. Any results we get are exciting but may not be convincing evidence if they aren't statistically significant in some way.

Most investigators are stoked about ITC devices like hack shacks, spirit boxes, pucks, and the ovilus. These devices are different in nature but all involve an entity speaking in real time through a calibrated machine designed for paranormal research.

I have a hack shack (or ghost box), which is an easily altered hand-held Radio Shack radio. It is an older model, as the newer Radio Shack radios are harder to configure for ghost box purposes. I have used it experimentally during research cases, although I have never used it in a client case due to its controversial nature.

....

Something to Know:
Occasionally, cell phone apps appear suggesting ITC experience, some even touting "ghost radar" capabilities. These apps are fun to play with and are for entertainment purposes only. It is unwise to use your cell phone as a piece of equipment during investigation, even for audio recording, as it can interfere with data collection. Teams often insist that cell phones be left at base or turned to "airplane mode" during investigation. As smartphones develop, there may come a time for them to play a unique, calibrated role on investigation—but not yet.

....

I am personally skeptical of radio sweep devices as well as pucks and the ovilus. That being said, I have been on research investigations where I've experimented with all three and they have all said very specific words relating to the investigation or people present. It is interesting, but I also feel that investigator psi may be able to affect these devices, so we do not know if it is really a spirit communicating or if an investigator may be subconsciously imprinting upon the device. Regardless, both options are intriguing!

I bring up the psi connection because some ITC researchers believe that a type of bonding (or imprinting) between the device and the researcher is almost a requirement. Patrick Burns, star of the cancelled show *Haunting Evidence*, swears by an old BlackBerry with audio recording capabilities. I've worked with Patrick and his cracked-up BlackBerry, and I can attest that the device gets loads of audio evidence. There may be a vibrational bonding between an investigator and the equipment that facilitates spirit communication. Or, this may be psi as the root of whatever evidence is captured. Or, another concept is the imprinting becomes an amplifier for real spirit communication to occur—meaning that the device itself is only one part of the puzzle and that our own energy is needed to complete the process. I'm just throwing these ideas out there for discussion; I honestly do not know how such things work. What I do know is that "talking" ITC devices are able to provide investigators with an instant bond to whatever may be present based on what investigators believe they are hearing. And while many consider the evidence questionable, ITC results provide interesting tales.

Unique ITC Considerations

I have a friend who has a deeply personal, beautiful ITC story. Fellow writer and researcher April Slaughter has one of those amazing personal experiences that really bring out the potential of ITC work. She is someone I know to be a credible researcher with a profoundly transformative story that took place because of an ITC device. This event hinges on another seminal ITC researcher conducting groundbreaking work.

In *Paranormal Obsession: America's Fascination with Ghosts & Hauntings, Spooks & Spirits*, I discuss researcher Andy Coppock's ITC device, which modulates EMF rather than using radio frequencies. He has intriguing success with this device. His device is unique for a few reasons. On the practical side of things, his device eliminates a lot of the static noise found with hack shacks. One may hear a buzz as an entity approaches but further interaction is often very clear, and the voice that comes through resonates like that of the living. The voices are normally clear as the radio dial garble is absent.

The device's history is interesting as well. Mr. Coppock first used a prototype while working with a severely autistic child who, her parents believed, was communicating with her recently departed grandfather. Andy was there during one of these events and clearly heard through the machine a type of data transfer between the child and some unseen presence.

His first thought was not so much about ghosts but about reversing the process so the device could assists communication-challenged autistic children. He took the device to a school for autistic children where a friend taught. To his amazement, he found the students responded positively to his invention. Andy and his research colleague, Michelle Brown, have continued to work on the device for ghost research while also devoting private funds toward how this device may assist children with autism and seizure disorders. The paranormal isn't always about woo-woo stuff!

Because Andy and Michelle are discreet about their work many don't know about the beautiful stories emerging from their research. My friend April was fortunate enough to experience their device. The event enhanced her own research and offered her an amazing glimpse into another world.

Here is what happened: April spoke with her departed grandfather in real time. What made this event so astounding is that the conversation wasn't generic—he addressed specific concerns about her children that she had never revealed to anyone. This incident, coupled with her own research, has caused her to deeply think about the role of ITC.

April is a respected up-and-coming researcher. I wanted to get her take on ITC work in general. I threw a few questions at her:

What appeals to you about ITC work rather than basic EVP research, for example?

ITC communication is with ghosts and spirits via use of electronic devices. This differs from EVP in that the communication is not only heard upon playback of a session recording, but in real time as it occurs. The responses are often instantaneous. This makes the interaction more personal and easier to continue for a sustained length of time.

What are some limitations to ITC research?

As with any other experimentation within the paranormal field, ITC is not a guaranteed phenomenon. It requires a large amount of patience and a finely tuned ear. Your results depend largely upon your openness to the communication, as well as the type of device you are attempting to use to establish a connection. Understanding how any particular device works is important as is the time you invest working with it. In my experience, one must spend time "imprinting" with whatever piece of equipment they intend to use. It is a rare occurrence for me to experiment with a new device and instantly achieve results. However, it is not always impossible either. I have also noticed that aside from one particular incident, I have never been able to maintain a connection and converse with any spirit/entity for longer than a few minutes.

Do you feel ITC research allows for nonhumans (inhumans, or earth spirits) to communicate as well?

Yes. I believe I have had contact with entities that were not the spirits of the dead. They have either identified themselves as something different, or have simply given me the impression that they have never been human. Do I know for certain that this is the case? No. It is entirely subjective.

How does ITC work, namely ghost boxes/spirit boxes? I'm not looking for a technical answer, but more of a metaphysical one. Why not any other device?

This is how I like to think of it: Imagine walking into a room full of people, and screaming at the top of your lungs without anyone even noticing you are there. You scream and scream, and then one person turns to ask you, "What's wrong?" You would talk to that person, wouldn't you? I imagine it can be rather frustrating for spirits/entities to speak with the living, especially when we are not actively listening for them or when we pass our experiences off as a product of our imaginations. When people begin working with ITC, it would seem that they put out the signal they are there and willing to listen. Obviously, the energy wishing to come through has to establish a certain amount of trust in the individual to try as well. The various ghost box devices, in my estimation, seem to make communication a bit easier for all involved. Spirits have told me that they themselves don't understand exactly how it works, but they are delighted when it does.

In your opinion, what are some ethical considerations regarding ITC work?

ITC, when successful, is an experience unlike any other. Throughout the years, I have seen other researchers and investigators become obsessed with the communication, spending much of their time working with ITC and neglecting other responsibilities. It is imperative that people learn the appropriate time to "hang up the phone" and remember that they have a life to live and things to accomplish outside of communicating with the other side.

Some people suggest that one has to "bond" with an
ITC device to get good results. What is that process about?

Yes, as I mentioned above, I believe "imprinting" with the device in use is important. It is not always necessary, but most of the more profound experiences I have had have been with devices I have worked with over a lengthy period of time. When I hold or touch the devices, they often react to me in an audible way. An amplified signal or static will emanate from the device before, during, and even after communication occurs. I am lending my energy to the process, often by means of meditation or deep concentration. I have found that mood definitely affects the outcome of any given session. You attract the energy that you put out, so I try not to work with ITC if I am not in a relaxed state of mind. Imprinting is a process unique to every individual, so there really isn't a protocol for doing it correctly.

Some also say ITC work, like mediumship, is best
facilitated with spirit guides or someone on the other side.
How do you feel about this?

While I believe this is often the case, it is not *always* the case. Some people (and even some devices) seem to attract particular spirits/energies to assist them in facilitating conversations. They may be present during many of the ITC sessions or just a few every now and again. I believe they enjoy being helpful when they can, but as with anything in the paranormal, it doesn't always happen because we desire it or on our timeline.

Does one almost have to develop an "ear"
for deciphering ITC recorded evidence?

With some of the devices, yes. Especially when working with those that utilize white noise or radio transmissions. It can be rather overwhelming and tiresome to work with them because it is hard to separate genuine spirit communication from the noise. In my experience, when contact is made and a conversation begins, I can *feel* it is something significant. Listening for words and sentences is helpful, sure, but the physical reaction I have to the sound is an indication that I should be paying attention.

In your opinion, what are some basic procedures for using ITC in research?

1. Be patient.

2. Remain open-minded.

3. Be specific in your requests. (e.g., who you'd like to speak to, that they use their voice to let you know they are there and willing to communicate, etc.)

4. Record the session with a digital voice recorder or video camera to capture any phenomena that may occur.

5. Organize your recordings and catalog all relevant information such as date, time, and surroundings.

12: Analyzing Data (EVP, ITC, and from Video)

I am not a very technical person. I enjoy philosophy and theory more than numbers and figures. But part of creating good data is knowing how things work on the technical end. Investigators need to have some knowledge of these things if we want to have others take our work seriously.

We have looked at basic EVP work and some considerations regarding ITC research. It is great to have hours and hours of audio, but what is the most efficient way to analyze all of it?

I consulted Steve Fernino, a friend, investigator, and professional DJ who knows a thing or two about sound.

Recording Techniques

Here is a rundown of Steve's most important points. He isn't the only one who has made these recommendations, but he took the time to send me a long email so I'm giving him a shout-out on this one.

Recordings should be captured using a *lossless* format such as .wav (the most common). You may also commonly see .pcm (which basically uses the .wav or .aiff formats). Lossy formats like .mp3 and .wma are more commonly used, but should actually not be used at all. Recording in these file formats actually diminishes audio quality as part of their compression to shrink file size. This is done by removing parts of the audio and leaving gaps that our brains "fill in" using our natural, hard-wired tendencies to find patterns in sounds. In other words, it creates audio pareidolia.

If using lossy formats, you may have already added false artifacts to a recording that you didn't hear during the investigation, manufactured by that format and by that format alone.

Record in 24-bit instead of the standard 16-bit resolution. These are not options for .mp3 or .wma, which is another reason not to record in those formats. Think of it as editing a photo or video on a computer. The higher the resolution, the more "pixels" (in this case, bits) you have to work with, the less it gets distorted, and the cleaner it looks or sounds. By using a higher bit resolution, you can process the audio a little more while altering the original audio less. You could go even higher than 24-bit, but Steve doesn't think this is necessary for our purposes.

A built-in high-pass filter (confusingly also known as a low-cut filter) will let you roll off some of the lower frequencies. Steve believes this is essential and should always be done at the time of recording, not during editing. One does not want to overprocess an audio file afterwards.

Steve recommends using the Zoom H2 digital audio recorder on its most sensitive setting, recording in .wav at 24-bit, and using the built-in low-cut filter. With this model, a lot of the heavy lifting of sound clean-up is already done. This setting can also be used with any higher-end model.

Review Techniques

The first thing Steve recommends is that you really need to have appropriate headphones to analyze any audio, regardless if it is obtained from a digital audio recorder or video.

He tells me to brace myself for a longwinded answer.

"To start, the brand of headphones is not as important as the type," he says. "On many of the para-reality TV shows I see people using cheap ear buds or small, cheap headphones. Neither of these are optimal."

Steve explains that there are two best types to use. The first is full-size closed-back headphones. These fit over the entire ear and use a closed-back earpiece that isolates the listener from a lot of outside noise.

The second type is in-ear headphones, particularly the kind used for in-ear monitoring systems. These are similar to ear buds, but are designed for greater isolation, comfort, and hearing protection. Because they insert in your ear canal, they provide superior isolation in the higher frequency ranges than closed-back headphones (which is why they are used for hearing protection and used by performers on loud stages). They also tend to have better overall sound quality than ear buds, which is a plus for EVP work.

The choice is more a matter of preference. Some people don't like wearing bulky headphones, while others feel uncomfortable with something inside their ears. A good pair of closed-back headphones that cover the entire ear will be fine for most and does a good enough job of keeping a lot of outside room noise at bay. If outside noise is a huge problem or you just want the best isolation and/or smallest device, in-ear headphones will be best as they simply block most sounds from entering the ear canal.

"I highly recommend not purchasing models with noise-cancellation. Unfortunately all noise-cancelling headphones and ear buds (even the highest quality and most expensive) produce some sort of audio artifacts that are then added to what you hear in the recording," Steve points out.

"[Noise-cancellation technology] produces false positives, pareidolia, or even the masking of proper EVP! (Active noise cancellation is an artificial process mimicking the naturally occurrence of what is called phase cancellation.) Also while most noise-cancelling works fairly well for lower to mid frequencies, it does not perform well for upper-mid or high frequencies, which is an important range for EVP work and the human voice alike. When using a properly isolated pair of closed-back or in-ear headphones without noise cancellation, no sound artifacts are created trying to isolate any exterior noise," he explains.

He recommends the Sennheiser, Shure, Sony, or AKG brands of headphones. He reiterates that one must look for headphones that are closed-back (not open-back), fit over the entire ear, are designed for "monitoring" instead of "general" listening, and have no noise cancellation. For an affordable, quality closed-back pair of headphones, he recommends the Sennheiser HD 280 PRO or Shure SRH440, both of which run around $99. For something even better, upgrade to the Sennheiser HD 380 PRO or Shure SRH840, which cost about $199.

Wow. I bet you never thought headphones were so complicated!

Software

I asked Steve what software he thought was good for EVP analysis. He recommends Audacity as one of the best programs for most people who do EVP work. It is easy to use, open-source (free), always improving, and works with Windows, Mac, or Linux. Mac users can use Garageband's powerful resources as well.

Adobe Audition is the top dog of audio editing software, but is expensive at $349 (both Windows and Mac). It is so good that some may not accept any evidence edited on Adobe Audition. (Britt Griffith of *Ghost Hunters* commented during a public lecture that any audio TAPS receives in Adobe Audition is always discarded because the file cannot be analyzed for alteration. If you use higher-end software like

Adobe, always keep another copy of the file in a different format for another program.)

Audition is made to be very powerful but also streamlined so it can be useful for professionals and novices alike. Many useful tools for EVP cleanup and editing are built in, but they may be overkill for an average user. If you learn how to use the features effectively, it is the most powerful and flexible tool out there, period. Another plus is that it fully integrates with Adobe Premiere, their amazing video editing software which makes a great combination for the audio and video work necessary in paranormal work. Audition and Premiere (along with Photoshop) can also be purchased in bundle suite form for a hefty $1699. This price is beyond what most investigators are able to spend or meaningfully engage, but it well worth the money for those who can afford it and learn to use it properly.

Steve throws in some bonus advice. "What I recommend doing is segmenting your recording during investigations by periodically pausing and hitting record again (which creates a new track). Maybe even throw in a verbal time stamp before you stop it and after you start it again. This is always a good practice anyway," he says before explaining why.

"When most digital audio recording devices lose power abruptly during recording, anything that hasn't finished recording is lost. If you had just recorded for hours continuously, it's likely all gone. However, if you had already paused the recording and began recording again, only what was on the current recording section may be lost," Steve suggests.

But how does one actually use the software for EVP work? The prevailing logic is that one should "clean" up EVP in audio editing software. However, your EVP may be compromised.

Steve suggests that when doing audio cleanup, it's never really a case of "use this or that." Every case scenario will require a different amount of cleaning up. The process is largely trial and error with the correct tools. But here is something that's always true: less is more. If something needs huge amounts of processing, throw it out. If a file only needs to be slightly enhanced, it is a keeper.

He explains what happens if one has to clean up EVP too much. "The EVP gets so altered that artifacts creep in and potential pareidolia and other issues become factors. It is also more likely that much of what needs to be cleaned up could have been addressed during the recording process through using the recorder's built in features and proper recording techniques and settings such as the high-pass filter, for example."

"So what are the proper recording techniques?" I asked. "Because these things are the most important measure you can take to maximize how the software is used for EVP analysis."

Steve clues me in on what he calls his "best-kept secret": The Levelator. It is a free piece of software designed for podcasters (Windows and Mac). He becomes giddy as he explains, "All you do is drag and drop your audio file (edited as a clip but not processed in any way) on to the Levelator (it only works with lossless .wav or .aiff formats). It uses a complex algorithm to adjust the levels of the file manually by analyzing the sample and automatically balancing various audio levels and the standard overall volume of the clip. It mimics the complicated and often destructive processes of compression, limiting, and normalization without many of the associated artifacts. When it is done, it creates a new copy and leaves the original intact."

He started recommending the Levelator for EVP work in the belief that we deal with the same frequency range as voice podcasts. He admits that while it has a good track record, it isn't perfect. Sometimes you will chose to use the Levelated version while other times the original sounds less altered or better. Use it with voice only, never try to use it with music or lots of weird nonvocal sounds, as it is not designed to optimize for that. The Levelator can be found at conversationsnetwork.org.

Be careful not to overprocess your audio file. Steve says that other editing in the world of professional audio "can be extremely useful if used correctly and in small doses, but when used incorrectly, can destroy the audio or even create artifacts that were never present in the first place, creating false positives and matrixing." Steve shares the same sentiment as many when he suggests that any findings altered heavily with any of these techniques should never be used as evidence.

Steve also stresses that one should always keep an original unedited copy of the file and create a new "working" file. Also, don't be afraid to learn what different things do to alter the audio, even badly. It helps in learning to correctly use it as well as to learn what not to do and to be able to identify artifacts introduced in other people's EVP.

13: Reviewing Photography and Video Data

I'm having coffee with fine art photographer Norah Hoover. She is not a paranormal investigator, but she tells stories with her camera and happens to live at a haunted artists' collaborative called Elsewhere in Greensboro, North Carolina. I wanted to catch up with someone who knows more about cameras than they do about ghosts, because the key to catching a credible ghost photo is knowing the camera's limitations.

Norah knows a little bit about spirit photography. We look at some famous online photos of ghosts. She points out that most ghost photos (credible ones, at least) are vernacular photos—a fine art term for casual, unopposed everyday photography—or found objects, as she likes to call them. When we think about it, the most famous spirit photography does not come from investigations but everyday, run-of-the mill snapshots.

"Found object" is the perfect term for summarizing what happens when someone snaps a great ghost photo. And snapping that great ghost photo is rare. Many investigators today may not take photos during an investigation at all for many reasons. For one, there are often plenty of digital video cameras surveying the investigation. Second, it is so easy to fake a ghost photo that a real one will be hard to pass off as authentic.

Yet cameras have a unique role in paranormal investigation and remain a popular entry-level technical tool. Norah details how initial ghosts reports from Spiritualism involved sound. "It was the rapping, or the rattling of chains that people associated with ghosts," she says. But technology advanced and then the camera—the visual component—became the medium, she points out.

Today, digital cameras dominate the field of investigation, taking the place of film. For that reason, I will limit my discussion to digital technology. I will not get into too much detail about how digital photography works; that information is readily available elsewhere.

I ask Norah how best to use a camera to catch a ghost. She then makes a statement that investigators rarely think about: "Well, it depends on how you expect the ghost to act."

We peruse some ghost photos online from different eras. She pointed something out. "You see how ghost photography has changed throughout time? It is because technology has changed, and it is easier to fake or manipulate images." Norah is not too impressed with some of the most famous ghost photos I show her. "It's just too easy to fake," she says. She is a believer in ghosts, but as stated earlier, she knows what a camera can and cannot do.

One way to effectively use photography is to document the area before an investigation. Some historic locations may ask you to do just that, particularly if there are valuables present. Panoramic photos of locations with the lights on provide useful reference for any photographed anomalies you may later capture.

I personally believe that cameras are best for debunking and documenting the environment rather than capturing convincing evidence. I understand this statement disrupts a long legacy of photographic use in paranormal research. Likewise, the camera is entry-level technology for many enthusiasts. My hesitation around relying extensively or exclusively on photography for investigation centers around three aspects: most people do not know how to use cameras, most cameras used by investigators are lower-end and produce too much photographic "noise" that can be mistaken for paranormal, and lastly, the age of Photoshop and fun smartphone apps makes it too easy to fake a photo.

That being said, I do not want to undermine photography's unique history by suggesting we dump it. On the contrary, it needs to find a place. As I previously stated, I believe photographs can be used to document a location with the lights on prior to an investigation. Additionally, it is fine to use a photographer, but designate someone to do it who has either a good camera or technical knowledge of photography. Too many people jumping around taking pictures is a distraction and possible contamination.

Here are some basic rules outlined by other authors like Joshua Warren and Troy Taylor. Many teams use these protocols or similar ones. Likewise, many of these techniques may also be applied to video.

- Take at least three pictures in a row: an establishing shot and two others.

- Depending on the context, alert investigators of "flash" before taking the first picture. I have been on investigations where everyone has a camera and this "flash" business served as contamination. Therefore, it is wise to designate cameras to certain investigators in the field to avoid this problem.

- Tried and true advice: make sure that the lens are clean, avoid getting the camera strap in the way, and be mindful of your hair, cigarette smoke, and breath.

- Note environmental conditions when taking photos, particularly humidity, moisture, and dusty conditions.

- Do not flash directly into IR bulbs of your digital video system.

- Be mindful of reflective surfaces.

- Keep some sort of log, either written or verbal, regarding time and location of pictures.

- Make sure your shutter speed is adjusted appropriately for photographing under whatever conditions you are in.

- Silence your camera from making any beeping sounds.

- Any camera will do, but lower-end models will produce more orbs. Invest in a SLR (single lens reflex) camera if you are serious about taking quality, usable images. A good SLR may also inspire you to be more of a photographer outside of investigation too.

- Mount the camera on a tripod to avoid unwanted jerks or motion. Even a handheld tripod is useful.

- Learn about shutter speed, IOS, and F/Stop functions on your camera. You will learn how to take credible pictures both on and off investigation. Discovering how to alter the settings unlocks new potential for your camera.

Chris Balzano points out great techniques for evaluation pictures in his aptly titled book *Picture Yourself Capturing Ghosts on Film*. He suggests some simple rules for evaluation photos. Don't spend too much time on an individual photo. Be sure to note the context around whatever was going on when you took a photo. Evaluate the photo with an open, non-paranormal mind. Be overly critical of what you've captured. Share your data with others for peer review and expect to be questioned. And if you see a light moving around (on video or captured on still photographer), try to find the source.

Here is an experiment: open your shutter and increase your exposure time. Have someone slowly dance around in front of the camera. Look at your image. You will laugh because you'll see a blurry, fuzzy, or otherwise ghostly apparition of your friend. Remember this the next time you catch such a photo.

Orbs?

It pains me to even have to write this, as the orb debate seems like a bad cold one can never shake. As said earlier, technology alters the very definition of the paranormal, starting with the "Orb Theory" debate spurred in the early 1990s when digital photography became accessible to the masses.

Today, it is widely agreed that most digitally photographed orb pictures are not paranormal in any capacity. Lower-end model digital camera create orbs that are most likely dust, mold, moisture, or other fragments. I would be cautious of any orb photo captured with a non-SLR camera.

Personally, I am frustrated with the whole orb thing. I have received cases where people are genuinely frightened because they photographed orbs in their home. In one instance in particular, the orbs lined up with the edge of their flat-screen TV. These two "orbs" were obviously a flash reflection off of that particularly glossy surface. The clients were convinced a negative entity was present.

Light anomalies are sometimes associated with paranormal activity and are occasionally witnessed in person. There are energy orbs that are not necessary paranormal. Ball lighting is one example, and natural gas "lights" such as the Brown Mountain Lights in North Carolina are another. These are naturally occurring anomalies not associated with ghosts despite the folklore that may have emerged to explain the phenomena.

It is true that some paranormal cases include light anomalies and it is equally possible for them to be captured on film or video. Körner's Folly's very first investigation involved several investigators seeing a bright flash of light that was later captured on video. It is not possible for us to surmise if it was paranormal, but it coincided with visuals, equipment malfunction, and an EVP.

Dr. Barry Taff photographed light anomalies during a case that later inspired *The Entity* movie. The lights were witnessed by multiple observers, captured on still photography, and in daylight. So one cannot suggest that cameras never get evidence—or that one has to be in the dark. It is, as always, about luck, timing, and knowing exactly how to use your camera.

The orb debate, however, is not sufficient scientific proof of any real spirit activity. Even if an orb is an energy orb, we cannot surmise it is a ghost. Orb photos remain popular in spite of this because 1) orb pictures are easy to take, fake, and replicate 2) for many, such photos provide instant proof a "ghost" 3) most people value the ghostly experience, such as the orb photo, more than they do the process of understanding real activity. Some want orb photos to be special. They may make great stories, and stories are good. Orb photos, however, do not make good science.

Chris Balzano summed this up perfectly in private correspondence:

"The mass of bad ghost pictures come from people who have the ability to afford the technology to capture images but not the training to know how to capture them correctly. More importantly, those images take on importance and get put out there because the people who take them want badly to have seen a ghost."

Infrared (IR) and Full Spectrum Photography

Photography offers a great example of how technology has enhanced and transformed what we understand about the paranormal. As I pointed out earlier, I am not as excited about photographic evidence as I am about other types (even video or audio) because too few know how to use a camera, and evidence can be easily faked.

However, I want to touch on this because IR and full spectrum photography may provide more credible evidence than previously available.

Many people are familiar with ghost pictures captured by Barry Fitzgerald using his Fuji full spectrum camera. Most shows have featured such technology, and prices are dropping to make it affordable for those who do not have production company budgets at their disposal.

IR and full spectrum photography access a part of the light spectrum that falls outside of visible light. Children, it seems, may pick up more of the light spectrum realm due to the eye's design, which alters a bit as we age. It is hypothesized that energies are more likely visible in the IR or full spectrum range because they vibrate at that frequency. Full spectrum use is becoming viable in forensics, a methodology that may be useful for ghost hunters. Small handheld full spectrum video camcorders are currently under $300—in some cases, cheaper. However, these models are not what viewers see used on television, which have undergone several hundred dollars' worth of modification.

The most affordable and accessible IR cameras are motion-sensitive hunting cameras. Starting at around $100 on the cheap end, they are static cameras that can snap a digital IR photo when something moves in front of it. I know a college professor (perfectly sane!) who took a series of photos in a daylit field. The sun caused the photos to have a pinkish hue. In one photo was a man-shaped mass that was not present in the photo taken before or after. It is an interesting anomaly that is hard to explain. Images on these devices are stored digitally and can be downloaded into your computer, which means they can still be easily manipulated. I will say that no matter how interesting and accessible these types of technologies may be to the average buyer, I have yet to hear of anyone catching something truly phenomenal. These devices are wonderful to have and fun for experimentation, but I am unsure how many questions technology may really be able to answer.

Video Considerations

The same basic instructions for video apply for audio. Before we review basic technical issues, it is important to look at a few larger concepts before buying an expensive (and possible insufficient) digital video recording system (DVR).

Most investigators hit an investigation with a handheld camera or an extensive DVR system. These things are sometimes useful, but not always. Ask yourself what you really hope to do with this equipment. Are you hoping to catch the world's greatest apparition? Are you trying to debunk? Maybe you're just trying to keep investigators under surveillance so you know where everyone is when you *do* get the most fabulous EVP ever.

I asked Chris Balzano his opinion. He expressed my sentiments, saying, "Video evidence can be useful but only if used the right way." Additionally, he is firmly against the use of any handheld video devices during an investigation. It's a hard statement to swallow for many investigators whose handheld equipment is the medium through which they see the world. Here is a back and forth:

Chris: I am bored of people showing their *Blair Witch* night vision clips to me and telling me the same random blink of light is a ghost. There is too much movement happening to get any real evidence, and the more advanced the camera, the less people know the effect of their bells and whistles.

Rebuttal: He has a point. I will say that my friends at AdventureMyths have come up with some good tips to avoid this jerkiness. One is to launch the camera on a handheld tripod, which gives you a bit more control. The second is to hold the camera up to your chest as you walk and investigate—with lens pointing outward, obviously, so you get a steady, frontal view similar to what the investigator is seeing. Again, one has to determine how to best use video on an investigation: to catch evidence or document investigators and the general environment.

Chris: From talking with investigators, watching evidence they get, and hearing their praise of media influences, it seems many get in an odd mindset when they turn on a video camera. They perform instead of investigate and lose focus on what they are doing (in more ways than one).

Rebuttal: Well, once again, it is hard to argue with this observation. If you are an investigator, video can be useful depending on your objective. But... if you are a legend tripper, video is a great way to document and tell your story. Regardless, both motivations require you to learn some basic filming skills and to know your camera settings. Again, my friends at AdventureMyths have not only learned cinematography skills, but they have also gained production and video editing abilities. They invested time, money, and talent into learning an entirely new skill set to enhance their investigative experience. Their objective is to document their investigation to create documentaries. You may not end up doing that, but basic filming skills can benefit everyone.

Chris: Some investigators spend so much time filming what they are doing, they lose contact with every other sense. The investigation becomes that one tool, or more precisely, they see the world through lenses rather than with their eyes.

Rebuttal: Yes, I have seen this happen with cameras and any other equipment used on investigation. We forget that our own perceptive skills are far more useful in assessing the environment than video. I endorse this statement for all equipment, which often becomes *the* experience itself.

Camcorders or DVR

Chris doesn't like handheld video cameras because most investigators produce jerky, useless footage. One way around that is to purchase a CCTV or DVR system. These are the rage these days, but they are an investment, and one has to know the kind to buy for investigative work. If you are looking into a good system, consider a variety of options. I thank Paul Browning for pointing this out:

- Frames per second (per DVR/per camera)—at least 30 fps *per camera* so your image is clear. If you want to catch evidence (shadow figures an apparitions), make sure your frames per second (fps) is high enough to matter
- Connector types: BNC/RCA
- Cabling: Decide with audio or without
- Live playback options
- Archive capabilities
- Camera's video resolution
- IR Capabilities (LED Counts)
- Cable lengths for each camera

Browning stresses that you have to consider a lot of options before sinking hundreds of dollars into a DVR system. The most expensive systems may not be what you need to catch apparitional evidence. DVR cameras often have iffy resolution unless you are prepared to spend top dollar.

Keep in mind that setup and break down of a DVR system takes time. Also, if you extend your DVR cable too much, the cable may become an antenna picking up other radio and broadcast waves in the environment.

Paul thinks one should invest in handheld cameras over a DVR system for a variety of reasons—but not so you can submit jerky footage. He says actually says investigators do NOT need to buy those expensive systems (which now run about $400-$600 in general, but may not include a monitor or extra cables). Handheld camcorders are fine provided investigators know how to use them. They have audio attached and do not always have to rely on power (as long as you have multiple batteries). Most camcorders now come with large internal hard drives or memory cards that make data storage external and upload easy. Paul points out that if your digital video recording system crashes, you lose everything. It happened to our team once: we were bad-mouthing writer O. Henry at Greensboro College and our DVR burned up while we were talking. Apparently, he haunts the place and takes offense when people speak ill of him. I cannot say if O. Henry had anything to do with it, but I can say that we lost all of our DVR footage from the evening.

One thing Browning points out about having camcorders instead of a DVR system is the equitable distribution of evidence review. This is what happens when a few investigators have most of the equipment, particularly video: they end up reviewing all the evidence. This isn't fair, to be honest. Keep in mind camcorder footage includes both video and audio, potentially meaning double evidence review time. If everyone has a camcorder set up (on a tripod), then review is equally shared.

I know some people put DVR footage on a CD or upload it to a server. More advanced groups may be able to do that, but not everyone has the capability to do so. Plus, you may have to convert the footage to view on your own computer. (I use a Mac and DVR footage always has to be converted for viewing.) Transfer of video files from DVR footage can become a headache.

One tool for converting is software called Dazzle. It is about $50 from some suppliers and is very useful to have. There is other software out there that may offer the same benefits, but I have heard fellow investigator specifically praise Dazzle (I do not get any profits from mentioning their name, I assure you). Any video will need to ultimately be in a universally accessible format (such as Quicktime) for viewing across multiple platforms. Just know that you may lose clarity the more you export footage to other formats.

There are multiple ways to use video on your investigations. It is important to think these things through before rushing out to buy tons of equipment. You don't want to be stuck reviewing thirty hours of evidence when your other teammates have only five.

Keep in mind that there are downsides to camcorders as well. Sony Night Vision used to be the gold standard in lights-out filming. There are rumors that they may be phasing out night vision capabilities on consumer models. Infrared extenders may not compensate for the loss of night-vision filming. This means that ghost hunters will have to send their cameras off for modifications, invest in higher-end models (expensive), or rely exclusively on DVR systems. Paul Browning reminded me that Bell Howell still has affordable camcorders with night-vision capabilities.

Changes in available technology may mean that investigators will have to learn new investigative habits. As Loyd Auerbach has always reminded us, most investigators investigate in the dark because that is what they see on TV. It hasn't always happened that way, nor is it necessary.

Best Use of Photography and Video Technology

I think the best use is not in efforts to collect evidence—although rejoice if you do. I believe photography and video are wonderful ways to document your environment and your investigators. For example, AdventureMyths set a camera up facing a haunted bathroom with a laser grid during their investigation at Historic Jordan Springs in Virginia. At 3 a.m., one sees several disturbances over a few seconds in part of the laser grid and a weird hum on the audio. This was on a static camera!

Another way to efficiently use handhelds is to document any ITC interaction, such as with a K-II meter or flashlight. Static cameras such as those used in DVR may not be able to zoom in and film, as the EMF meter is slowly climbing up to the number you requested.

One great way to really win kudos is to make sure that all investigators are in front of a camera during EVP sessions. This ensures that no one was making any noise or movement that may be misconstrued as an EVP.

Photography is useful for documenting the environment before the investigation. However, some investigators really bond with their cameras and enjoy using them in the field. That's great, but be sure there are some conditions and control in place for using photography during the actual investigation.

....

Something to Know:
Video and Photography Considerations

- Determine how you want to use your video system: To catch evidence or to document your investigators to make any evidence you get more credible? This determines what you purchase.

- Understand that for every hour of video you capture, it may result in double evidence review time, particularly if audio is attached. Keep this in mind—it determines how much time you spend reviewing evidence and how much storage space it takes up on your computer.

- Invest in good video viewing/editing software if your computer doesn't come with it.

- Make sure you understand the limitations of video and photographic equipment.

- Make sure those who purchase video and cameras understand how to use their equipment.

- If possible, have an outside professional videographer and photographer to provide an outside opinion. Many areas have amateur filmmakers' organizations with members who have extensive knowledge.

....

14: Effective Report Writing

We need to ask questions about what the world will say about paranormal investigation a hundred years from now. Will the academic community have long forgotten parapsychology and ghostly phenomena? Will the thousands of investigators today go on to other hobbies? Or will we see *Ghost Hunters* and *Ghost Adventurers: The Geriatric Version*, with Jason Hawes and Zak Bagans battling it out with walkers and wheelchairs?

Jokes aside, we will probably see many entertainment cycles between now and then, but the real question is this: What will your work accomplish for the future? Perhaps you will become a YouTube star or maybe you will have fifteen seconds of fame guest-starring on a new reality TV show. There is no other historical moment where so much investigation has taking place. The challenge is whether it is making a difference in the long run—if you are contributing to the condition of knowledge. We like to think we are, but I'm unsure if most teams are really taking that extra step.

That extra step that many of us skip is documentation. It's not fun, it's not glamorous, and many people don't think much about it because they don't see it on TV. But if we want to preserve our data and investigative efforts for future generations, the very first, most basic step is to start collecting a body of literature. The easiest way to do that is in solid report writing.

I am a writer so I like to write. I may be good at it on occasion. But not everyone enjoys putting ideas on paper, and I understand that. So don't worry if you aren't a writer—I'm including two different types of reports that serve as examples of how to put a report together. You can always recruit someone for your team who has writing skills. And remember, the following reports are really thorough. Yours do not have to be this comprehensive.

Keep in mind that residential reports may be different. For example, we have a team report that may include psychic impressions, but we rarely share those with the client unless the impressions resulted in tangible evidence or historical information.

What you include in the report is up to you. It is acceptable and increasingly common to have a multimedia report that includes video, audio, photographic, and other evidence. But one can't completely bypass the written report. For one thing, those multimedia file formats may be obsolete in a few years (like, say, floppy disk and now probably DVD and CD). The written word is always the root.

Here are two sample reports. One is long and involves many types of evidence, including psychic impressions. The other is case specific and more direct in nature. Both report styles serve a purpose and provide excellent examples of how to write reports.

Sample Report:
Haunted North Carolina, Victor Small House (Public Location), Clinton, NC

This is one example of a report. Note that only investigator initials are used. We argued about the inclusion of investigator impressions, as we normally do not share those with the client. However, part of this investigation included an amended version of the Gertrude Schmeidler study I discuss in the next chapter. This is a great way to see how it was incorporated.

Investigation Report, 8 October 2009

Victor R. Small House/Sampson County Arts Council

GPS Coordinates: Longitude: -78.3174; Latitude: 35.0018

Natural Area Code: 8G65T NT08B

Investigation date: Friday, 18 September 2009 at 3:00 pm EST

Weather: Relative Humidity 58%; Barometer: 30.11; Temperature: 76F

Moon Phase: New Moon

Solar/Geomagnetic Fields: Solar X-rays: Normal

Geomagnetic Field: Quiet

On the night of 18–19 September 2009, the investigative branch of Haunted North Carolina, Inc., (hereafter "HNC") conducted a six-hour investigation with the primary intention of identifying and documenting paranormal activity at the above location. Since the client did not report any specific manifestations, no debunking of reported activity was required.

The investigation commenced at roughly 9:30 pm with HNC's ongoing research into the possible correlation of (1) perceptions of spirit activity among persons identifying as "sensitive," (2) ditto, persons identifying as "nonsensitive" (a.k.a "controls"), (3) measurements of electromagnetic fields and temperatures immediately prior to the investigation, and

(4) history of reported paranormal activity by witness accounts, including data from an investigation conducted a year earlier by Triangle Paranormal Investigations of Clayton, North Carolina. This study is modeled after the work of Dr. Gertrude Schmeidler, and is similar to studies currently being conducted by the Windbridge Institute of Tucson, Arizona, and others. This phase of our investigation is a work-in-progress, and is therefore not discussed herein.

At 11:00 pm, video cameras were employed in several locations historically regarded as active, and baseline photographs of the entire building were made. By 11:45 pm, three teams of five persons each began a series of Electronic Voice Phenomena (EVP) sessions in various locations within the Victor R. Small's Home and Medical Practice Building.

ACTIVITY REPORTED
Note of caution: Many EVP are quite subtle, and should be audited with headphones.

Doctor's Waiting Room and Office
A large number of EVP were captured in these two rooms during the entire course of the investigation, but most are hardly or completely indiscernible, for example:

- AUDIO FILE: HNC_Office_EVP1.wav: 7 seconds in, a distinct whisper, saying something like "skin hand cut" or "Steven Hancock."

- AUDIO FILE: HNC_Office_EVP2.wav: 4 seconds in, a hoarse female voice, possibly saying "Sit down."

- AUDIO FILE: HNC_Office_EVP3.wav: Sounds like, "I'm feeling fine."

- AUDIO FILE: HNC_Office_EVP4.wav: Investigator asks, "Where do they belong?" A man's voice whispers something sounding like "Hector."

EVP: At about 10:00, male and female "psychic" investigators entered the waiting room from the entrance door to begin the psychic walk-through. As they entered, a female voice was captured that possibly says, "Evening, sir." The female investigator spoke immediately after, indicating that she is not the source of this voice.

• AUDIO FILE: HNC_Office_EVP5.wav

EVP: An anomalous voice was captured, which might be that of Dr. Small, given the content of the text, "Leave her alone. This is my house. She's always been around here." We have three recordings of this EVP, but they are not identical. One of our investigators identified her own voice as saying, "They leave her alone. (pause) Uh. She's always been around here." But what happens during the pause in the two other recordings is curious; the phrase "This is my house" is apparently the same voice, yet it did not emanate from our investigator! I am providing you with a sound clip of all three, first from the speaker herself, which lacks the phrase "This is my house," then from the two other recordings, in which the phrase "This is my house" is clearly audible.

I had reservations about presenting this as evidence, so I sent it to an EVP authority for his opinion. He replied, "I agree with you that there's an anomalous voice in there. It's not clear which one is the real person and which is extra. My sense is that #2 and #3 contain a whispering voice that is masked on #1 by the speaker's voice."

• AUDIO FILE: HNC_Office_This Is My House.wav

ITC (Instrumental trans-communication): Another method we use to try to establish communication, through equipment that can be manipulated by a spirit. In the following instance, a flashlight was turned on with its battery cap loosened, so that minimal intervention (vibration?) would cause the light to vary from off to on. Because it is a LED flashlight with several lamps in it, the amount of light emanating from it is variable.

We experienced a seemingly interactive yes/no dialogue that lasted about four minutes. We cannot, however, explain how nor guarantee that this is in fact what is happening. Note that variations in the amount of light changed in conjunction with our line of questioning. This occurred at 2:45 am in the doctor's waiting room, as shown in the following video recording.

- AUDIO FILE: Waiting room; Small House, Clinton flashlight.wav (sent by mail on CD-ROM)

Physical sensations: Other phenomena experienced by multiple investigators in this area of the house are sensations of light-headedness and other symptoms of illness. Of course, the power of suggestion relating to a doctor's office may be a trigger, but the quantity and nature of such experiences are worth noting.

"As we were sitting in Dr. Small's office during the EVP session, I felt a very distinct feeling of congestion in my lungs and the need to cough. I had not felt that way nor did I feel that way again for the rest of the night. I remarked that it felt like someone was trying to give me the impression of tuberculosis." FH-HNC

"I became extremely dizzy and disoriented as we walked through the medical offices. The sensations were so strong, I had a difficult time functioning." IC-HNC

Susan, a representative of the Arts Council who accompanied us on this investigation, stated that she felt light-headed as she entered the waiting room early that evening. And I [Steve Barrell] felt sickly when I sat in a corner of Dr. Small's office, a place where another investigator had first sat, then moved from for this very reason.

Back Stairs

1. During the first EVP session, an investigator remarked, "Oh. I just heard Matt or Matthew in my ear." The whisper was not picked up by our recording devices. Since all investigators came into the investigation with no prior access to or knowledge of historical information, she could not have known that the house was owned by a Mr.

Leamon Matthews, who killed himself in the bathtub situated near the back stairs.

2. Just as one of our psychics said, "I was just about to say the little girl wanted to send a marble down the stairs," a flashlight directly in front of me [Steve Barrell] moved and continued to rock. I make a point of not moving—unless absolutely necessary—during EVP sessions, in order to minimize noise. I had no reason to reach for the flashlight, except spontaneously once it moved, to stop it from rocking. I cannot say with absolute certainly that I did not jostle the flashlight. I include this incident because an identical incident occurred during the TPI investigation, when a voice recorder was knocked off the back stairs, which suggests a pattern of kinetic activity.

Upstairs Bathroom

EVP: While a team was working in the bathroom, an investigator noted the sound of someone approaching. The following recording captures a few sounds, including a raspy (possibly female) voice. There is difference of opinion as to what was said, from "It's 9:45" (it was 12:45 at the time), to "Let me find some light." The voice is not that of an investigator. I leave it to you to decide what you think is being said.

• AUDIO FILE: HNC_Bathroom_EVP1.wav

Main Floor Parlor (Piano Room)

EVP: Shortly after midnight, members of Team 1 were discussing the height of a young girl who touches people on the forearms, a phenomenon that occurred during the TPI investigation as well as being reported by visitors to the Small House, including a Clinton artist who first told me about the Small House. In the following EVP, a girl seems to say "Get 'em," followed by three chuckles simultaneously as a female investigator speaks.

• AUDIO FILE: HNC_Parlor_EVP1.wav

EVP of Whistling: The sound of whistling was captured twice, by two investigators on separate equipment, shortly after midnight during the HNC investigation. It is extraordinarily unusual and out of protocol for investigators to whistle during an investigation, and such a thing would not go unnoticed. Moreover, both recordings were recorded just several few minutes apart in the Piano Room:

• AUDIO FILE: HNC_Parlor_Whistle_EVP2.wav

• AUDIO FILE: HNC_Parlor_Whistle_EVP3.wav

I recalled capturing two EVP of whistling, also in the parlor, during last year's TPI investigation in which I participated. Most remarkable is that three of them, one from HNC and two from TPI, begin on exactly the same pitch, and one consists of two entire musical phrases, clearly indicating that the source is not a squeaking door, etc. I am, however, unable to identify the tune. The following audio excerpt is a compilation of all four instances of whistling: HNC / TPI / TPI / HNC

• AUDIO FILE: HNC_Parlor_Whistling_4X.wav

EVP—Music?: Two investigators were alone in the music room during the psychic impression walkthrough sessions, when they captured this very curious, perhaps musical sound, which occurs about 3 seconds into the audio clip.

• AUDIO FILE: HNC_Parlor_EVP4.wav

Other Manifestations: Being Touched On The Forearm

Several investigators reported the presence of and being touched by a young girl.

• "A little girl who held my hand and touched my arm, she kept wanting to be next to me for company and comfort. In the front parlor on the left as you face the house. She huddled up to my left arm and side as I was sitting in a chair and held my hand as well. She tends to stay downstairs in the house or in the medical building. She also came to me and held my hand when I was in the doctor's office doing an EVP session." DD-HNC

- "I had the feeling of being touched on the forearm in the front room when we were setting up equipment." FH-HNC

- "I was touched numerous times during our investigation." SH-HNC

- "I saw moving shadows multiple times throughout the night and felt as if I was touched on the arm and back of the head multiple times." TW-HNC

- "Liz also felt it, a child was in the [piano] room, an adult just entered and is watching. Liz's arm is being touched." SB & LE-TPI

Appraisal

In my opinion, there is sufficient EVP evidence to support assertions of paranormal activity at the Victor R. Small House, in Clinton, NC. Although we were unable to capture any photographic or video data to suggest paranormal phenomena, we captured a convincing body of EVP recordings that include whistling, music, whispers, and speaking voices. With regard to personal experiences, I am not inclined to justify an opinion regarding paranormal activity based on perceptions and sensations, but I include this information in this report because of its persistence.

Thank you for permitting Haunted North Carolina to investigate the Victor R. Small House. We look forward to continuing our relationship with the Sampson Arts Council. Please do not hesitate to contact us.

Respectfully submitted,
Haunted North Carolina, Inc.

Sample Report:
Fort Stanwix, Scientific Paranormal, New York

Here is another shorter report from Scientific Paranormal. This report is more precise in dealing with specific claims. Their team representative pointed out they aim to do a few specific things in their report:

- Address the claims of the client, our attempts to debunk them, and our conclusion about them (or lack thereof);

- Describe any personal experiences our team had during the investigation;

- Present any video or audio evidence we captured and our opinion on it; and

- Summarize and offer our conclusions and recommendations to the client.

- The client receives this report along with all evidence clips. In addition, the team will call or meet him or her to discuss it.

Investigation: Fort Stanwix

Date(s): 9/10/10

CLIENT ACTIVITY CLAIMS AND ANALYSIS:

1. *Client Claim 1:* Apparition of a boy running between Gregg and Tiebout rooms

   RESOLUTION: INCONCLUSIVE—The Scientific Paranormal (SP) team did not find any data that would suggest an apparition of a boy down this area. We had one infrared DVR camera and a full spectrum camcorder focusing on this area. Neither picked up any unusual visual activity. This is not to say that no apparition may be appearing here, but that we were unable to validate this claim. There were no other objects that would make someone believe an apparition was there, so it is unknown why someone would make this claim.

2. *Client Claim 2:* EMF activity in the courtyard

   RESOLUTION: INCONCLUSIVE/NATURAL—The SP team found no unusual EMF fluctuations or spikes in the courtyard; however, it should be noted that various electrical wires nearby can produce EMF bursts, which can register on EMF sensors. For example, in the General's quarters, an EMF burst was detected whereby an area registered a high EMF then it dissipated. This can be anything from a high electrical signal to cell phone reception. In addition, several buildings had natural high EMF from the electrical wiring, which can also contribute to this activity.

3. *Client Claim 3:* EVP found in commandant quarters reported by a staff member recorded on a cell phone

   RESOLUTION: INCONCLUSIVE—The SP team investigated the commander quarters extensively. While we did not locate any EVP within this room, an investigator was poked in the head and she reacted strongly. This remains unexplained, but other possibilities of why she could be poked could be nearby bugs. Other possibilities of an EVP could be nearby voices picked up through either the outside or a nearby room. It should be noted that while no EVP's were found in this room, there were several unexplained noises and possible EVP's in the missionary room. (see below)

4. *Client Claim 4:* Knocking in missionary quarters

   RESOLUTION: NATURAL—The SP team found some evidence that this knocking heard on the wall from the missionary quarters was simply wind hitting the window against the side. An investigator mimicked this sound and was on the other side of the wall. When the window was slightly hitting the sides, it made a noise similar to a knocking on the wall. At this time, this claim is considered natural/debunked.

Scientific Paranormal Activity and Analysis

1. *SP Staff Personal Experience 1:* Shadow seen in end room in missionary quarters

   RESOLUTION: PARANORMAL/INCONCLUSIVE—
   This activity occurred when an investigator was walking past a room. Looking briefly into the room, the investigator saw a large shadow that blocked out part of the light through the room. Upon investigating what could cause this, the shadow was no longer there. Unfortunately our DVR infrared camera that was near this area was not positioned where the shadow was seen, so we could not validate this claim.

2. *SP Staff Personal Experience 2:* Faint light figure seen in outside parade grounds

   RESOLUTION: INCONCLUSIVE/NATURAL—This activity occurred while an investigation team was working on debunking the room with the loose window. One investigator was looking outside at this time and saw what appeared to be a humanoid figure walking past the parade grounds. Upon investigating this, there was no figure. We had two infrared DVR cameras watching the outside grounds. No figure was seen on cameras. Thus, we have determined to debunk this claim. However, it is mentioned in this report as we believe different lights from the outside Rome city, in combination with the grounds inside (and fog included), could create illusions of figures. While this is not necessarily what this investigator may have seen, it can be a strong possibility.

3. *SP Staff Personal Experience 3:* Female voice heard

   RESOLUTION: PARANORMAL/INCONCLUSIVE—
   This activity occurred when an investigator was packing
   up equipment at the end of the night. Walking past one
   building, the investigator heard a female voice. This voice
   was so clear that the investigator called to the rest of the
   team to determine if any female investigators were present
   in the building. However, there were none. No audio
   was present in this building, and most nearby audios
   either were removed at this point or not close enough to
   detect this voice.

4. *SP Staff Personal Experience 4:* Investigator being poked

   RESOLUTION: PARANORMAL/INCONCLUSIVE—This
   activity occurred when an investigator was working in
   the General's quarters and felt a heavy poke on her head.
   She immediately reacted and began searching for
   something that could have poked her, such as an object or
   a bug. None were found and none were recorded on
   DVR. At this time, the reason why she felt she was poked
   remains unknown. While some bugs were present in the
   area, there were no bugs found near her on DVR at the
   moment of her being poked. Also there were no objects
   near her that could poke her.

Paranormal Evidence Found

1. *FS_dooropen.wav:* This is a clip that was taken when a
   staff member of Fort Stanwix was beginning his rounds
   of closing up the area and locking doors. This audio was
   still present in one room in the family quarters. While
   the door is heard being latched, about 7 minutes later,
   the door is heard being unlatched and opening up as a
   dragging sound is heard. There are no other footsteps
   before or after this door opens up. It is unknown if this
   door was simply blown open on its own or if the door

itself was completely unlatched. The latter would be difficult to do, although not impossible if the latch was not placed on properly.

2. *FS_familyqclip1.wav:* This is a clip that was on the same recorder and location as the above one. About five minutes later, as the team begins to wander near this area to break down equipment and close up for the night, a whisper that is out of place is heard. This whisper appears to say "She's" or "Peace," but it is uncertain. A "clean" version is presented here to isolate the potential EVP. Please note the surrounding noise is normal distorted sound as a side effect from the noise removal, it may appear louder than the original clip.

3. *FS_missionary1_mobile.wav:* This is a clip that an investigator found also in the missionary quarters. When an investigator asks, "Why don't you show yourself to us?" a low moan is heard. However, there is much debate on if this voice is a unique voice to the group or if it is a lower voice either nearby or outside of the area.

Natural Evidence Found

1. *FS_missionary_knock(debunk).wav:* This is a clip that was done to debunk the banging heard on the wall in the missionary room. One investigator was moving the window to the room slightly to mimic wind. When the window hit the side panel, a rumble such as a bang was heard. The walls between the two rooms are very thin, and thus someone on the other side of the room could easily mistake this as a knock on the wall when in fact it is just wind knocking against the window.

History of Location:

Fort Stanwix was built in 1762 under British General John Stanwix. Originally, the Fort was an important neutral treaty ground where the British and the Iroquois Indian Nation negotiated terms. The Fort eventually was abandoned in 1768 after the treaty was signed. In 1776 the Fort was reoccupied by Colonial troops under Colonel Elias Dayton. Technically, the fort was renamed Fort Schuyler for a time. The Fort saw a siege on August 3rd, 1777 under a combination of British forces and Native Americans. While the Fort was taken back over by the British regiment, a nearby skirmish, The Battle of Oriskany, forced the British to withdraw from the Fort. Two combined American forces, one led by General Benedict Arnold, forced the British forces away from the area completely. The remaining forces went north to Fort Ticonderoga. The Fort burned to the ground on May 13th, 1781 due to a combination of heavy rains and fire. General Washington decided to abandon the Fort completely. However, the site was eventually reconstructed between 1874 and 1978 after it was designated a national historic landmark.

CONCLUSIONS:

The SP team found moderate but not conclusive data that supports a paranormal event in Fort Stanwix. Some of the claims were either debunked or more logical explanations were presented. In addition, some of the personal experiences that our team had logical natural explanations to them. We had thirteen infrared digital video cameras throughout the entire Fort complex. Through all of that footage, we did not capture any unnatural video activity. However, our audios did capture some unusual clips in the form of possible object sounds, moans, and perhaps a voice. It should be mentioned that these audio clips are still under review and debate if they are natural or paranormal, which puts them in an "ambiguous" category. In this category the clips are not counted as highly as clips that are deemed paranormal, but are not thrown out entirely either. Combined with our personal experiences, audio data found, but lack of conclusive evidence, the team believes that there is not enough data to support the presence of paranormal activity at the Fort. However, if a paranormal event is occurring, it would be more likely in the form of a "residual haunting," meaning that paranormal activity occurs randomly and without intelligent thought. This type of haunting makes it difficult to interact with as the activity would be unaware of our presence there. As the Fort itself has burned down, and a reconstructed model is over it, this would also support this type of haunting as any residual activity might remain in the foundation.

The SP team would recommend additional investigative research into this area to better narrow down and determine what may be going on here. More time would be needed in the Fort and farther into the night in order to gain more data to support or refute the possibility of a paranormal event. The SP team would be happy to return at any time to the Fort if new claims are determined or if additional research is requested.

If you have any further questions or concerns about your case or data, please do not hesitate to contact us. Thank you.

Sincerely,

Scientific Paranormal Management

As you can see, these two reports use very different styles and formats but are thorough and professionally presented. The first report included extensive explanation of techniques, theories, and psychic impressions. The second was claim specific and provided debunking perspectives. How you form your report is up to you and your methods, but having something well written and concise can go a long way in creating a body of literature.

Data Management

It is increasingly becoming important to know how to manage your data, particularly as investigations now involve multiple devices and multimedia components.

As I pointed out, the first component is to document your investigation in writing through a solid final report. But you also need to think about how to systematically reference, save, and archive your data.

Teams need to come up with a standardized file-naming system for all data, including word documents, EVP, audio, and photography. Both sample reports included different file naming systems. In the Victor Small House example, some EVP files were saved like this:

• HNC_Office_EVP2.wav

This denotes the team, the location, and the fact that more than one audio artifact was collected. One can use this similar format for video (.mov files) or for pictures (.jpg files).

Scientific Paranormal uses a slightly different format:

• FS_dooropen.wav

The FS denotes the site, Fort Stanwix, and the location of where the clip was captured.

Standardized file naming is great for final reports and is beneficial if you find a format and stick to it. But you may want to consider using a different internal format before final report status.

We often ask investigators to name files with their initials, location, and time stamp. It makes for a long file name but easy reference during review regarding (1) who captured the EVP, (2) where it was captured, and (3) the approximate time for crosschecking. A file example may look like this:

• DKS_KFRecRoom_1014.wav

This means that Deonna Kelli Sayed captured this EVP in Körner's Folly's reception room at approximately 10:14 pm. A similar file format is also recommend by ATransC.

It is generally not recommend to name your EVP file after what you think the EVP is saying, such as this: getout.wav. This automatically biases any listener to what it may say. Remember the EVP study I referenced early in the book? It is often hard for outsiders to reach a consensus on EVP, so it is best to let other investigators and clients hear it first before suggesting what might have been said.

When it comes to video, I would ask the client what sort of computer he or she has and make sure DVR and other video footage can be viewed with its software. Always ask what type of computer a client has.

Data sharing among team members may be another challenge. Some teams have servers or computers dedicated to storing and sharing data, but not everyone can swing that. Some use Yahoo! groups as team-member-only sites to upload photos or EVP, but storage is limited. Dropbox is a free online data storage system, but it is free only up to 2 gigabytes; video, audio, and photographic data will eat it up in no time.

I recommend that individual investigators—team-based or not—come up with a personal, systematic way to save data long term for posterity. To date, there is no centralized archive or repository protecting data and reports for future researches. It is all up to you and me.

15: Research Design— Thinking Beyond the TV Shows

Most investigations today revolve around debunking and EVP work. This can be challenging and fun. But after some time, the same old EVP routine gets old. You long for something new. And research demands new thinking—in some cases, revisiting the old literature to implement what parapsychologists were doing before reality TV.

I enjoy investigation, but I am often bored with the same routine. I want to learn something new and expand my boundaries. At some point, you will too. Perhaps you will gravitate toward experimental equipment. Or you may get creative with your video documentation. Maybe you want to do some documented research and experimentation. If you want to do research, it's important we discuss just how to do it.

Scientific Method

No ghost-hunting book is complete without a shout-out to the scientific method, about which there is much talk. Most residential cases may not need "science" as much as they need some advice. In fact, one can't always do things in a "scientific" manner in a client's home because the situation does not call for it. But one must always try to find alternative explanations and use deductive thinking in all cases.

The basic tenets of the scientific method are something most fifth-graders can recite by heart, but worth reviewing here.

The first step is characterizations or observations. For our purposes, we can call these "case claims." The second step is to formulate a hypothesis based on the claims. We mentally do this whether we admit it or not. We either hypothesize that there is a ghost, that there are natural explanations at play, or the client and witnesses need psychological help. When someone says they are going in as a skeptic, their automatic hypothesis is that there IS no ghost. What investigators normally ask at this stage is, "What could be going on in this home?" with some preconceived possibilities already in their minds.

The third step is testing what we believe to be the case. This means going into a home to debunk or ask EVP questions (the act of asking means that we hypothesize, at some level, that something is there to talk back). We are testing our hypotheses at this stage.

Data analysis is the next step. For some, this is the end point. But in scientific inquiry, this is a crossroads. We may indeed uncover strong evidence of, say, Aunt Bertie hanging around because she loves her little nephew, but it is generally rare to get such tangible evidence. We have to reformulate our hypotheses based on what we do—or do not—capture.

Paranormal research is one of those fields that doesn't often shore up evidence to match its hypotheses. And, unlike more traditional areas of science, it is rare that we can repeat an event when we do get evidence.

But if we do get evidence, we need to have it peer reviewed. This may mean having people on your team who weren't on the investigation that night to have a listen or a look. Or it may mean sending it off to others off-team. And in a completely ideal world, you could go back to the site and try to get the results again.

But the ghost frontier is hardly ideal. So we have to be creative in how we use scientific thought. I have a friend who is a professor and a paranormal investigator. We will call him "the Prof" because he keeps his ghost job out of his day job. His day job is at a university where he spends a great deal of time working with statistics. (He spends his nights seeking ghosts and his days dealing with numbers and figures. What a paradox!)

The Prof says that statistics can actually be useful, sort of, in ghostly research. He brought up a great concept that few in the paranormal community discuss: the null hypothesis.

Here is how the null hypothesis works. A kid goes up to his teacher and says he can't find his book report, which he assures the teacher was completed but has mysteriously disappeared.

"In my hypothesis," the student claims, "my report was abducted by aliens. After all, it was on secret government UFO intelligence."

The teacher replies that while she finds that hypothesis intriguing, "the null hypothesis is that your book report was *not* abducted by aliens." Then she asks him to prove his alternative hypothesis that aliens did in fact steal it. The only way of supporting his hypotheses is to refute the null.

In cases like this (ghostly phenomenon) we select a null hypothesis. It sounds more complicated than it is. The Prof clears it up: "For example, we begin with the hypothesis that there is no paranormal activity in a location. When reviewing data, we see a five-foot tripod slide across the floor while no one is in the building. How likely is that to happen under the null hypothesis that there is no paranormal activity?"

Statisticians can usually quantify these likelihoods (at least under certain assumptions). But when it comes to the paranormal work, all we can say is that a ghost is pretty unlikely. Could it be that something natural moved the tripod five feet? Sure!

The Prof continues: "There could be a localized earthquake or something. Maybe a pipe burst in the floor directly under the tripod and rattled it. It is always possible there is a natural explanation, but under a statistically oriented scientific approach, we would reject the null if the probability is below some threshold, such as 5 percent or 1 percent."

Investigators then need to ask whether they think the likelihood of this tripod moving on its own is less than 1 percent? "Statistically, I would say it is probably far less than that," Prof interjects. "Therefore, from a purely scientific perspective (in my view), we have to reject the null hypothesis that there is no paranormal activity."

He takes it a step further. "What is *not* a scientific approach is to say that there must be a natural explanation because ghosts do not exist. This presupposes what we are trying to test. Sadly, this is the view of most who would call themselves scientific."

The Prof doesn't stop there (this is why I try to avoid talking to people who really know statistics. I get a headache.). "Now, the catch is that we reject the null in favor (at least in one theory of hypothesis testing) of an alternative. But in our investigative work, the alternative just has to be that something unexplained happened. We can't say it is a ghost or what it is with any certainty." Of course, that is incredible frustrating for us.

Hopefully I haven't lost you; I only want to mention that we are trying to collect "data," but obviously the data we are obtaining isn't collected in a controlled environment. In statistics, this type of data demands special consideration.

The Prof explains that "the statistical view of the world says that we can never really prove or disprove anything. We can only say by appealing to data that some things are more likely than others."

I had a great conversation with a university professor (not the Prof) who is also a closeted paranormal investigator. I once asked him if he really thinks we are obtaining evidence of ghosts. "Well," he said, "I don't know about that, but I do believe we are obtaining data that something intriguing is going on." I think this is a great way to discuss it. We don't really know if we are dealing with ghosts, PK, or quantum consciousness (or all three), but we do know we are getting some unexplained data. Yet not having solid answers is frustrating when you want to help homeowners.

The Prof agrees that bridging the scientific and human parts is challenging. And as I said earlier, pure science does not always cut it when dealing with a client. "Helping the client may be another story. It may mean telling them what we think is going on and what they can do about it, even though we cannot scientifically prove what we are saying."

Despite his statistics background, he insists that his "main purpose is to help the clients, and these two goals may not match up. There is the research aspect and the human aspect. My method is scientific (at least to a point), but the human aspect is the point of it all."

Most investigators will find that they have to adapt to the human aspect (helping people) and the research aspect (doing science) working together. This is part of the journey and when you do research, it is helpful to have some help in designing your experiments.

Psychic Impression Experiment

If you read the report from the Victor Small House, you saw a study mentioned by parapsychologists Gertrude Schmeidler and Thelma Moss. The report revealed how we used it on investigation.

One of its components involves another nuanced study having to do with psychics and investigators choosing a list of terms that fit or contradict their impressions. This assessment was initially meant for psychics or those with paranormal sensitivity, but Loyd Auerbach believes that any individual who has experienced activity should participate. It is best used when witnessed can complete this sort questionnaire separately from one another, then the team can compare notes, so to speak, to see in what ways individual perceptions are similar.

Instructions: Ask witnesses (or your own team members or sensitives during their walkthrough) to circle words they feel represent a ghost's activity. In the original study, participants were asked to cross out any terms they felt contradicted their impressions, and to leave any words alone that were not applicable. To simplify, create a chart or list of adjectives that describe emotions, movement, or physical descriptions of any entities or energies. Add your own words too. The objective is to have everyone do this little walkthrough, preferably at a location where the claims aren't known to investigators. Afterwards, compare note to see if anything correlates:

> **Sample lists (easier to read if in table format):**
>
> • *Impressions of emotions:* happy, sad, confused, lonely, playful, frightened, mischievous, angry, bored, fearful, protective
>
> • *Impressions of behavior:* walking, sitting, standing, lying down, dancing, singing, eating, playing an instrument, repairing something, communicating, puttering around, wandering aimlessly, hiding
>
> • *Impressions of other attributes:* crying, playing games, shy, trapped, nonthinking, walking, moving in a definite direction

You get the idea—create a long list of words, ask participants to cross out things they didn't pick up on, and circle words they felt made sense. It is not necessary to ask people to describe physical characteristics of an entity (child, man, woman) unless you want to. Remember, some people will pick up on different emotions or behaviors rather than actual mental pictures.

Psi and EVP Experiment:
Major Graham Mansion

In the hills about twenty miles east of Radford, Virginia is a gravel road that travels deep into the woods. The road crosses rolling streams, a quaint abandoned mill, and a deer-filled forest. When you come around the bend, you'll find a stately home at a place called Cedar Run. It is called Major Graham Mansion, and the large estate includes remarkably well-preserved slave quarters, two springhouses, and a barn. It strikes a commanding presence, and according to the Virginia Paranormal Society, it is possibly paranormally active.

Major Graham Mansion has a complex history of gothic southern Civil War proportions. An Irish immigrant named Squire David Graham purchased the land in the early 1800s. The location had a bewitched history even at that time. Slaves allegedly murdered the previous owner on the site in the late 1700s, and in turn were hanged on the property.

Squire David built Major Graham Mansion and moved his wife, Martha Bell, into the home. The marriage was not considered to be a good one. Research suggests that Squire David may have hit the bottle too hard and that his wife suffered from depression.

Their firstborn son, Major David Graham, the home's namesake, was born in the house in 1838. He lived in the house his entire life and served as a lieutenant in the Civil War. The attic floor of the house includes what is called the "Confederate Room" with a secret panel that some believe was used to conduct military meetings during the war years. It is quite a contrast to the basement of the home, which includes a shackle room thought to have confined disobedient slaves. There is an upstairs classroom where Major Graham's daughter taught local children during the Civil War, and this room is considered to be one of the more active spots in the home.

The mansion passed into the hands of other colorful personalities, including a man named Reid Fulton who enjoyed walking around nude. This law professor owned Major Graham from the 1940s until the late

1970s. The home was listed in the National Registry of Historic Places in 1984.

The current owner has made many restorative efforts and launched Graham's Fest, a local music festival scheduled to reappear this year. There are other public events planned for this sprawling property, including a new outdoor stage. Major Graham also offers paranormal-themed events and the owner enjoys sharing the estate's spirited history.

Virginia Paranormal Society was the first to investigate the property and knows it well. They arranged for us to have an experimental investigation. We had Major Graham for a whole night, so we decided to get busy with a variety of experiments testing psi and EVP work. Again, the following shows a way to make investigation fun, meaningful, and research-based.

Major Graham Investigation/Psi Experiments

The Major Graham investigation will consist of one passive experiment, three or four active experiments centered on capturing EVP, and exploring the role of psi/telepathy in investigation regarding EVP-related evidence.

BASIC PROTOCOL

- Investigators must be in front of a camera during all EVP work.

- Evidence must be reviewed in full and a written report submitted to the appropriate person by _____.

- Investigators should arrive around 2:30 pm. Those unfamiliar with the property will take a walk-through of the layout of the home to record impressions. A short tour will then take place.

- EVP experiments should begin no later than 4 pm.

REQUIRED EQUIPMENT

- All digital audio devices

- Handheld camcorders and tripods (if you own one)
- EMF/Mel Meters/Trifield Meters (if you own one)
- Earphones
- Notepad/pen

Passive Experiment

A series of varying digital audio recorders will be left in an unmolested location for a duration of three hours to see what device best captures EVP, if any at all. An investigator will need to verbally tag the time every 45 minutes.

Psi/Telepathy EVP Experiment (Active Experiments)

The objective of the Psi/Telepathy EVP Experiment is to establish if psi/telepathy is a contributing factor in the collection of Electronic Voice Phenomena (EVP). This experiment may indicate the role of psi in some capacity, but will not be able to pinpoint the exact mechanism of psi-related captured EVP. It is impossible to know if EVP is related to the Experimenter Effect or evidence of a "soul" via survival after death, although such repeated long-term experiments may help to eliminate certain variables.

Design

The experiment comprises six twenty-minute EVP sessions, three of which involves different "sitters" who mentally ask a set of questions.

The questions will consist of a prepared set of forty numbered questions on note cards, with two blank questions. The cards will be shuffled and organized into two sets of twenty questions.

During sessions with the sitter, s/he will remain in view of the camera with twenty prepared questions on notecards. The notecards will have the number clearly marked on the back. The sitter will verbally announce the number of question being asked ("Question one, Question fifteen," etc.). The sitter will then mentally read the question several times, wait sixty seconds, then move on to the next question. Blank note cards will be treated as a "nonquestion" and allotted sixty seconds as well. The sitters will be two females and one male, and will include at least one person who identifies as sensitive.

Alternatively, there will be three "control" sessions with different participants verbally asking twenty questions from the prepared forty. Participants will read a question out loud, wait thirty seconds, and then proceed to the next question. All participants must be in view of a camera at all times. The sitter(s) will NOT be part of the control group.

A Trifield meter will be in the room in an effort to correlate any environmental changes.

Approximate time: 120 minutes

Equipment: Camcorder, at least one digital audio recorder, Trifield meter ideally placed in view of camera, timer (can be cell phone if put in airplane mode).

"Secret Word" Psi Experiment

During a predetermined allotted time (from 5–7 pm, for example), investigators will mentally assert individual, established "secret words" during EVP sessions. The objective is to see if any such words emerge as EVP. Investigators should NOT ask EVP questions related to their own secret word, nor should investigators share their word with others during the investigation.

Prior to the allotted time, participants will each determine their own secret word and write it on a piece of paper and insert in a sealed envelope. Investigators will write his/her name on the envelope and hand it over to one individual who will open and compile a list of investigator-word AFTER the investigation has completed.

EVP Bursts

This experiment will test the hypothesis that EVP occurs in long gaps between questions.

Design

Four individuals will conduct a series of four three-to-five-minute EVP sessions. Data will promptly be reviewed on sight. This will be conducted with three rotating teams in a pre-assigned location.

Approximate time: 20 minutes each session/ 60 minutes
Equipment: digital audio recorders, earphones, timer
Location: Slaves Quarters

GHOST BOX SESSION

This experiment will see if the Ghost Box is (1) is a valuable field investigation tool and (2) perception and interpretation of "results."

Design

Two twenty-minute group sessions with the Ghost Box. This will work as a traditional EVP session where investigators ask questions with 15–30 seconds between. This can also take place during the Secret Word experiment.

Approximate time: 40 minutes
Equipment: Camcorder and digital audio recorders

TRADITIONAL EVP/INVESTIGATION SESSIONS

Groups may rotate through selected areas of the property conducting twenty-minute EVP work.

What did we learn from this? For starters, it is hard for people to sit for forty minutes and remember if they are to verbalize or mentally ask the question. Most sitters did not wait for the full minute required between questions although we had a clock present. That is OK—but it shows that this experiment may be best shortened. Loyd Auerbach pointed out that it is advisable to have a known sensitive or psychic as a control (as that person may be better able to "imprint" EVP). We also designed some questions to be gibberish or even to have colors and shapes to see if a ghost can read. Results of this particularly test were inconclusive.

EVP bursts can be useful for immediate review. However, keep in mind that reviewing the data can take up to three times as long as the short bursts, and we spent more time in a very chilly environment comparing possible EVP than we did doing any work. We obtained one EVP from the slave quarters literally twenty seconds into the first blast.

This is just one example of how to design a research-based investigation. There are many other options. One may use experimental equipment, for example, or other mediums (literally). All research is useful.

However, you need to document the heck out of everything. Write it down. If writing is not your strong suit, find someone on the team who can create really well-written reports. They don't have to look like what's in this book, but they should be done with care.

Dowsing Rod Experiment: Mineral Springs Hotel

Mineral Springs Hotel in Alton, Illinois is considered to be the most haunted building in a haunted town, according to Troy Taylor. It was originally the site of a meat packing plant, and a hotel was built on the property in 1914. As with many older hotels, the site allegedly experienced murder, intrigue, and fantastical spirit stories that Taylor suggests may be more fiction than fact. Nonetheless, there are reports of activity on the site and several accounts of activity, although few match up with the prevailing legends. Taylor himself experienced spooky footsteps in the swimming pool area and others have heard the sounds of swimming although the pool has been water-free for years. He theorizes that the presence of underground water sources, such as the mineral springs, provides energy for hauntings.

As with many old grand hotels, Mineral Springs became less glamorous and saw more transient-type clientele by the 1960s. The location is now revived as an antique mall. There are haunted tours both in Alton and at the hotel, including one organized and researched by Taylor himself. Some friends of mine conducted a neat experiment at the site and have allowed me to share it here.

There is often a perception that one needs cool equipment to conduct experimental research. You've seen relatively low-tech examples as one way to use methodological approaches. Technology certainly adds a useful layer, provided you know how to use the equipment and analyze and correlate any data captured.

I heard of a simple yet methodologically sound experiment using dowsing. Kim Risinger, founder of Paranormal Encounters of Mid America (PEMA), shared how they developed this experiment:

Two dowsers were set up in a location in the Mineral Springs Hotel called Pearl's room. One facilitator also asked questions during the session.

All three people sat in a straight line approximately four and a half feet from one another. The dowsers were ten feet apart from one another and rods were not visible to the other dowser but in full view of the facilitator, who sat in the middle in full view of both dowsers.

They started the session by introducing themselves and explained that they were there to chat. A simple demonstration was presented regarding how the dowsing rods work. The sitters asked whatever spirits attended to cross the rods for yes and make them stay straight for no.

The facilitator asked approximately twenty questions. The dowsing rods moved in the exact same way in fourteen out of the twenty questions, or 70 percent of the time.

They believed they were communicating with an eight-year-old named Cassandra, who is thought to be the spirit of an eight-year-old girl who drowned in one of the hotel's pools known as the "men's pool." Several teams have apparently captured this information through EVP and ITC devices. Cassandra is thought to be the most social of the spirits at that location.

At the end of the session the facilitator asked, "When the rods did not cross in the same way, Cassandra, were you playing with us?" At that time, everyone's rods crossed to indicate "yes."

As an anecdote, the dowsers then suggested to Cassandra that she go into another room to "mess with the men" who were set up three floors down in the "men's pool area." Later in the evening, one of the men in that area mentioned that he had felt someone tug his pants.

They repeated this experiment three months later. This time, the facilitator asked approximately seventy questions. Again, the dowsers had their backs to one another and were sitting at a distance. Both sets of rods moved the same way forty-six out of seventy times, or 66 percent of the time. As before, they felt they were speaking with a little girl named Cassandra and again suggested she go mess with the men in another specific location.

Later in the evening, one man reported seeing what he explained to be a small pair of legs dangling over the side of a pool (as if they were soaking their feet). In addition, he thought he saw a stuffed teddy bear move right next to where he saw the apparition.

This experiment was simple and low-tech at an active location. What makes this methodologically sound? The fact that there was a procedure followed, and duplicated results, makes this interesting. Some could say a spirit's energy was moving the dowsing rods, while others suggest the two sitters may have had a telepathic connection (and one way to test this is to do this experiment with the same sitters in a nonactive location). Either way, these simple experiments point to the potential of something extraordinary possibly having occurred.

Things to Try Out on Your Own

Paul Browning wrote a book called *Thinking Outside the Box*. In it, he shares some interesting ideas that are well worth promoting, at least for experimental purposes.

I will say that the TV determines what many investigators do with their weekend haunt jaunts. It is a great way to enter investigation but an awfully boring place to stay. Staring at K-II meters waiting for the lights to go off is tiresome. Asking the same EVP questions location after location is often uneventful. Doing the same routine every time does little for innovation in the field.

At some point, you will find that EVP sessions get boring. You will want to do something more with your investigative experience. Residential client cases may require you do to certain things to assist the client. But there are moments that you may be able to expand your creativity and, well, think outside of the box.

Browning suggests that you type out instructions like "Move this chair" or "Open this door." Tape these instructions up at a location and put a camera on it. See what happens. We do not know if entities can read, but this is one great way to find out. Ideally, you would put up these instructions where activity is not known to occur. Otherwise, you will not be able to determine whether the door opening is due to spirit literacy or something else.

Another thing he suggests is a variation of something seen on one episode of *Paranormal State:* enter in costume. Browning adds that teammates should go in dressed as painters or acting as if the building is about to undergo renovation. The reasoning behind this is that activity seems to increase during construction or renovation on a property. He postulates that "setting up a stage" may also increase activity. This is obviously something the client needs to be in on, and discussing it beforehand in a house is discouraged in the event that ghosts can also listen in.

Trigger objects may be useful. HNC has experimented with laminated photos of some historical object or person relating to the site being investigated. Two or more such photos are placed in a room corner or on a table, ideally in an undisturbed area. Underneath the picture we place a large, fake gold coin. We traced the outside of the coin and ask whatever present to move the coin under whatever picture they may recognize or find significant. Ideally, cameras are set up to make sure an investigator doesn't purposely or accidentally disturb the site. Afterwards, we see if the coin has moved, indicated by the outline traced around it.

A friend of mine used a small breath mint box as a pillbox at a site that was a former hospital. Investigators there also wore white lab coats. The investigation was really productive, although it is hard to know if the attire helped. The point is to have fun and be creative. Share your ideas with others, because that is the only way we are going to learn.

16: Ethics

Personal Behavior

Paranormal investigators live to find evidence. The better ones strive to debunk it. The best ones (well, in my opinion) try to do all that *and* theorize the mechanism behind the evidence. The most honorable ones try to help people understand it.

Reality TV has changed everything when it comes to ghost work. A serious discussion around ethics is needed to reflect the changing landscape of research and moral considerations. There are two components: The first is determining ethical evidence and behavior, meaning coming to some agreement about data we can meaningfully determine to be paranormal (suggesting there aren't any other nonghostly explanations). Attached to this is the responsibility investigators have to behave professionally out in the field, be it at historic locations or with clients in their homes.

The second part of this discussion concerns what we do with evidence after an investigation. Unfortunately, many teams steal evidence from others and pass it off as their own. Likewise, people have heated opinions over what makes something "evidence" in the first place and often behave as children when disagreement occurs.

I drove down to Florida during a holiday break with a neighbor, a retired surgical nurse. She does not have any profound interest in the paranormal although she has had a few experiences throughout her life.

I shared with her some cases where medical issues were real variables. For example, one person I know sent her husband out night after night to investigate strange noises she heard coming from her yard. This woman was convinced otherworldly beings were present. However, the next trip to her doctor revealed that she had stopped taking Effexor (medication for depression) and one side effect of quitting such meds cold turkey can be auditory and visual hallucinations. My neighbor was not crazy nor were there strange people outside; she just needed to ease off her meds slowly. I actually know of three separate instances where sudden cessation of Effexor caused paranormal-like experiences.

"Wow," my neighbor said. "I didn't know this component existed. You'd never know that watching those shows."

"Of course not," I explained. "There are times when investigators are the first people in a home where there may be undiagnosed medical, emotional, or psychological issues present. We may be the first people to recommend someone seek medical or professional help."

She thought about that for a moment. "So, in some ways, what you guys do is like crisis intervention? I never thought of it like that!" That label had never occurred to me, but she brought up a good point. In many ways, good teams are "first responders" to often desperate situations. I mean no disrespect to the first responders to horrific events like 9/11, for example. However, investigators who go into private homes may be the first people to document very serious health and emotional issues. We have an obligation to at least suggest the client seek help even if we are not legally or ethically able to diagnose their nonparanormal ailments.

A case claim once came in where a client suggested their infant was under physical demonic attack. We did not take this case nor did we have enough information to report the parents to social services. But this claim disturbed me on a variety of levels. Any infant exhibiting odd behavior needs to see a doctor. Any parent suggesting a child that age is under demonic attack needs to see a therapist. And should you ever have a case where any children present have marks on their bodies that their parents claim are demonic, the laws of your state may require you to anonymously report it as child abuse. Be prepared to assume this kind of responsibility. You are free to believe in demons and the like, but a lack of common sense should never cloud your judgment.

It really inspired me to hear my friend understand our work in the way that she did. If you do a private case, it is not always about the ghosts or spirits—it is about the people. Clients deserve to be treated with respect and always receive follow-up from your group, regardless of what you do or do not obtain on investigation.

Evidence

It is ethically necessary to take care in how we present the data we obtain. If we are honest with ourselves, our own personal beliefs and opinions come into play when we interpret any data.

I mentioned a particular EVP study, earlier in the book, conducted by Dr. Mark Leary. The study, "Consensus and Disagreement in the Interpretation of Electronic Voice Phenomena: The Ferry Plantation House EVP Project," serves as an example of how mindful investigators need to be regarding all data interpretation.

Dr. Leary points out that investigators often disagree about what an EVP may say. This disagreement raises the question of whether any one interpretation is correct. Assumptions we make about what EVP are saying may potentially "misinform investigators regarding the nature of paranormal activity, but reporting incorrect interpretations is misleading to clients and others," he writes.

The study featured over ninety-four EVP collected at the Ferry Planation House in Virginia Beach, Virginia. The EVP came from eleven investigators on seven different investigations. Dr. Leary threw in two non-EVP audio clips, such as him writing on a chalkboard.

Twenty-four individuals of both genders agreed to interpret the EVP. Most, with the exception of two, belonged to a paranormal team. They had the CD of clips, an interpretation form, and a background questionnaire about their own beliefs in the paranormal, television shows, and a brief measure of basic personality dimensions.

Out of ninety-six EVP, only one had 83 percent agreement on what was being said. As Dr. Leary discovered, the average agreements with a "consensus interpretation" was about 21 percent. He points out, "In other words, only one out of five raters listed an interpretation that agreed with the most common consensus interpretation." Some EVP had no consensus at all and interpretations varied wildly.

Dr. Leary concluded that all investigators, regardless of experience, needed to demonstrate less confidence in their interpretations of EVP than they typically do. His study demonstrated that most interpretations were not agreed upon or even close to a consensus. Keep in mind that these EVP samples were strong, clear examples.

This study demonstrates that investigators sometimes have blind confidence in their abilities to adequately assess any evidence, EVP or otherwise. While some may be more careful than others, most do not take time to assess their own objectivity in any data interpretation. This leads to ethical discussions on a variety of issues, including what constitutes real research and potentially misinforming clients on the nature of data collected in their homes.

Generally, best practices for evidence review is similar to what academics do with their work: blind peer reviews. This means that ideally, teams send those pictures, videos, and audio clips off to someone else who wasn't on the investigation without telling them what to look or listen for. External peer review of evidence is a hard call and not fun, but it can be very revealing.

Putting It Online

All groups have websites these days, and most want to post cool evidence for the world to see. Some investigators use twitter and Facebook every step of the way on investigation. This is where things get murky. I personally feel if you are at a fun, public location, it can be neat to tweet about the cold spot you just experienced. In my personal opinion, however, it is rather tacky to tweet from client homes. Be mindful of how much information you put up on social networking sites regarding private cases. And always make sure you have full, express permission from the client regarding what and where you post any evidence.

Here are some questions to ask:

- What is to be gained from posting information about an ongoing investigation online?

- Would the client or location feel uncomfortable if we post updates via social networking sites during an investigation?

- Do I have full permission from the client and/or the location to post any information online, including evidence?

- Regarding photos, do I have permission from those in the photo to post online (other investigators)?

- How will I feel if I post evidence online and then later find out that other teams are passing it off on their sites as their own?

Here's a general rule about using evidence that isn't yours: if you want to use another's team evidence as an example, please contact that team first and get express permission. Acknowledge the evidence source on your own site.

Standardization

There is a great deal of discussion these days about the need for "standards" in the field, for everything from ethical behavior to methodology and evidence.

Two basic ideas drive these discussions. The first is that there is no way we can set standards because we do not know what we are really dealing with in the first place. Are the phenomena ghost-related or merely creations of our own psi? There are also no criteria for who and what goes on in paranormal investigation. Anybody can do it, regardless of professional or academic background.

Some believe that setting standards may stifle creativity and experimentation. There is also the fact that creating (and enforcing) standards requires a group of people or an organization for monitoring; many feel that "policing the paranormal" is problematic and just plain wrong.

Another idea returns to scientific legitimacy: if we want the real research community to take our work seriously, we have to get serious. There needs to be at least one segment of the "field" that is standardized and populated with credible researchers. We aren't doing anything productive by not establishing some widespread protocol and documentation for future generations.

Both sides of the argument are valid, and there is much to be said for experimentation. I happen to think the paranormal community is extraordinary in the wide array of people who come together in its cause: plumbers, academics, school teachers, car mechanics. Remember, science as we know it did not begin in high places. It started with everyday people asking the right questions. It did not begin with standards, necessarily.

However, the reality is that today, research of merit needs to have established protocol and proper documentation. I advocate that there be a voluntary effort to standardize certain investigations. This means that investigators can come together for specific, research-related events where they mutually agree to follow a certain protocol. Or, teams may volunteer to adopt certain standardized protocol for their everyday operations and share data with other teams who have done the same. "Voluntary" is the operative word here, as some investigators do not care to advance science. They are interested only in legend tripping, and that is OK. Those in voluntary networks can agree to mentor each other through the process.

Your Rights

There is an emerging public side of this that did not exist previously—knowing how to protect your own interests and those of any clients you work with.

One new reality is the relationship between paranormal groups and public historic sites deemed haunted. I know several teams who have "discovered" new sites and mentored these locations as they entered onto the paranormal scene. Teams invested time and money conducting paranormal investigations and creating online promotional material for these locations. Maybe the team organized local media work and even some fundraising events for the site. I love it when paranormal investigators can benefit history and locations, in addition to residential clients. It is truly a way to give back.

Unfortunately, a disturbing trend is also emerging. Sites are opened and become locally popular. These locations start charging more and more for paranormal events and the teams who launched them become embarrassed. No one argues that public paranormal interest is a wonderful way to raise supplemental funds for historic locations. Yet the paranormal community has a strong, visceral reaction to overt greed. Sometimes it goes beyond even that. At times, teams have been asked to start paying for access, despite the hours they volunteered investigating and promoting the site.

In some instances, the site is ultimately featured on a TV show. The team who mentored the site is often disregarded and not mentioned even if their evidence is used. I know that the informality of the paranormal community is problematic, nor can anyone control what producers feature on a TV show, but I also feel that historic sites need to show some gratitude for the teams who help them gain paranormal publicity.

Here is some advice should you and your team happen upon a newly discovered public haunted location: consider drawing up a contract with the site that stipulates access conditions and rights to evidence attribution in any media endeavor. I acknowledge that new groups may never face this reality, but more established groups will understand what I am talking about. A contract covering several years, if possible, also protects the team in the event that site management changes to individuals who may not understand or appreciate the paranormal side of things. Note that a contract is not a foolproof way of protecting your interest, and it may be hard to enforce if one party backs out. But it is a great way to establish rapport and a long-term relationship with locations.

That being said, I will caution any team against insisting on exclusive rights to a location in terms of investigation. This is just as bad as historic sites gouging teams financially to investigate. A team may have some special privileges, particularly if they have worked hard to promote the location, but it is rather tasteless to insist that your team is the only one who can investigate a site. Be fair and be professional, and encourage locations and others you work with to do the same.

In the same vein of stressing professionalism towards others, fairness and professional manners also apply to team dynamics. Unfortunately, there are instances of sexual harassment and equipment theft between team members, for example. Personal jealousies sometimes undermine team dynamics, with clients and historic sites in the middle.

Final Words

Investigation is meant to be fun, personally meaningful, and intellectually challenging. Paranormal experiences are often cool or maybe frightening, but they are also mystical experiences. This means they can change lives and cause individuals to alter the way they view reality.

When you think about it, there is a lot at stake.

For many of us, doing this kind of thing is the only space in our lives for deep thinking. Investigation allows us to meaningfully engage those complex ideas about life, death, and personal reflection beyond what we do in our daily lives (except for the few of us with day jobs that require this type of thing). Ghost hunting, legend tripping, and paranormal investigation become a philosophical classroom, a church, a therapy couch, and a personal growth experience for many.

Behaving ethically is a key component of a dedicated investigator, regardless if one legend trips or enters private homes. Honoring history, both of the location and that of the larger field, is also a part of honoring ethics. This avocation may be a casual hobby or a lifestyle, but the call to responsibility is the same for all. You and I are now part of the story in different yet wonderful ways. There is room for all of us as long as we remain respectful of our clients, what we do, and each other. The human aspect is always the variable we must return to whether we are legend tripping, conducting scientific experiments, or helping homeowners.

I do the paranormal gig in my spare time. I even write books about it. It is essential, however, to realize that this endeavor is not the sum of the world.

I end here with a call for investigators of all persuasions to do no harm. Investigate ethically and joyfully, and let this journey take you where it may.

Bibliography

AdventureMyths, http://www.adventuremyths.com, accessed on July 15, 2011.

Association TransCommunication (ATransC), http://www.atransc.org, accessed on July 15, 2011.

Auerbach, Loyd. *ESP, Hauntings, and Poltergeists: A Parapsychologists Handbook.* New York: Warner Books, 1986.

———. *A Paranormal Casebook: Ghost Hunting in the New Millennium.* Dallas, TX: Atriad Press LLC, 2005.

———. *Ghost Hunting: How to Investigate the Paranormal.* Oakland, CA: Ronin Publishing, 2004.

Balzano, Christopher. *Picture Yourself Capturing Ghosts on Film.* Boston: Course Technology, 2010.

———. *Picture Yourself Ghost Hunting.* Boston: Course Technology, 2010.

Belanger, Jeff. *Communicating with the Dead: Reach Beyond the Grave.* Pompton Plains, NJ: New Page Books, 2008.

———. *Picture Yourself Legend Tripping: Your Complete Guide to Finding UFOs, Monsters, Ghosts, and Urban Legends in Your Own Backyard.* Boston: Cengage Learning, 2011.

Belanger, Michelle. *The Ghost Hunter's Survival Guide.* Woodbury, MN: Llewellyn Publications, 2010.

Blum, Deborah. *Ghost Hunters: William James and the Search for Scientific Proof of Life After Death.* New York: Penguin Press, 2006.

Browning, Paul. *Thinking Outside the Box.* LuLu.com, 2010.

Butler, Lisa. "French Sleep Experiment," AA-EVP News Journal, Summer 2002.

Finucane, R. C. *Ghosts: Appearances of the Dead and Cultural Transformation.* Amherst, NY: Prometheus Books, 1996.

Holzer, Hans. *Ghosts: True Encounters of the World Beyond.* New York: Black Dog & Levanthal Publishers, 2004.

The Harris Poll, "What People Do and Do Not Believe In." December, 2009.

Haunted North Carolina. http://www.hauntednc.com, accessed on September 10, 2011.

INSight Paranormal. http://www.insight.org, access on September 10, 2011.

Jones, Marie D. *PSIence: How New Discoveries in Quantum Physics and New Science May Explain the Existence of Paranormal Phenomena.* Pompton Plains, NJ: New Page Books, 2009.

Jones, Marie D. and Larry Flaxman. *The Resonance Key.* Pompton Plains, NJ: New Page Books, 2010.

Leary, Mark. "Consensus and Disagreement in the Interpretation of Electronic Voice Phenomena: The Ferry Plantation House EVP Project." Accessed on September 15, 2011, http://www.paranormalresourcealliance.org/Ferry_House_EVP_Report.pdf

MacRae, Alexander. "Report of an Anomalous Speech Products Experiment Inside a Double Screened Room," *Journal of the Society for Psychical Research,* 2003.

Pye, Michael, and Kirsten Dalley, eds. *Exposed, Uncovered, and Declassified: Ghosts, Spirits, and Hauntings. Am I Being Haunted?* Pompton Plains, NJ: New Page Books, 2011.

Rountree, David. *Paranormal Technology: Understanding the Science of Ghost Hunting.* New York: iUniverse, 2010.

Sayed, Deonna Kelli. *Paranormal Obsession: America's Fascination with Ghosts & Hauntings, Spooks & Spirits.* Woodbury, MN: Llewellyn Publications, 2011.

Schoch, Robert M., and Logan Yonavjak, eds. *The Parapsychological Revolution: A Concise Anthology of Paranormal and Psychical Research.* New York: Penguin Group, 2008.

Scientific Paranormal, http://www.scientificparanormal.com, accessed on August 13, 2011.

TAPS (The Atlantic Paranormal Society), http:///the-atlantic-paranormal-society.com, accessed on October 1, 2011.

Taff, Barry. *Aliens Above, Ghost Below: Explorations of the Unknown.* Harpers Ferry, WV: Cosmic Pantheon Press, 2010.

Taylor, Troy. *The Ghost Hunter's Guidebook.* Chicago: Whitechapel Productions, 1999.

Warren, Joshua P. *How To Hunt Ghosts: A Practical Guide.* New York: Fireside Books, 2003.

Index

G

Geomagnetic activity, 27

Ghosts, 5, 7–12, 16–17, 26, 29,
32–47, 49, 51, 55–56, 58,
61, 92, 115, 118, 124, 139,
145, 147–148, 150, 158–159,
171–172, 174–175, 205–207,
217, 221

Ghost Club of London, 44

Ghost Hunters, 9, 18, 23, 26,
38–39, 43, 48, 51, 53, 60, 65,
92, 96, 139, 147, 150, 155,
166, 177, 182, 185

Ghostvillage.com, 48–49, 63, 66

Going dark, 132–133

Grounding, 138

Guiley, Ellen Rosemary, 2, 17, 47

Griffith, Britt, 155, 166

Group culture, 3, 47, 60, 64, 68

H

Hawes, Jason, 9, 45, 47–48, 185

Haunted North Carolina, 1, 23,
113, 122, 125, 128, 187, 193

Historic Jordan Springs, 182

History, 1–3, 8, 14–15, 30, 36–40,
42, 48, 51–52, 57, 61, 70, 73,
77, 107–111, 114–115, 145,

154, 158, 173, 188, 198,
209–210, 225, 227

Historic sites, 66, 74, 77, 83,
94, 129, 225–226

Holographic theory of the
universe, 15

Holzer, Hans, 2, 11, 37

Hoover, Norah, 171

Human agent, 51

Human Consciousness, 4, 30

I

Imprints, 9–10, 148

Inhumans, 15, 17, 21, 160

Infrared, 132, 176, 182, 194,
196, 199

International Ghost Hunters
Society (IGHS), 48

International Paranormal
Investigators, 68

Internet, 37–38, 47, 52, 59, 62, 65,
83, 106, 109, 114

Insight Paranormal, 77–78

Instrumental
Transcommunication
Devices, 4

ITCs, 4, 21, 155

GET MORE AT LLEWELLYN.COM

Visit us online to browse hundreds of our books and decks, plus sign up to receive our e-newsletters and exclusive online offers.

- • **Free tarot readings** • **Spell-a-Day** • **Moon phases**
- • **Recipes, spells, and tips** • **Blogs** • **Encyclopedia**
- • **Author interviews, articles, and upcoming events**

GET SOCIAL WITH LLEWELLYN

Find us on
Facebook
www.Facebook.com/LlewellynBooks

Follow us on

www.Twitter.com/Llewellynbooks

GET BOOKS AT LLEWELLYN

LLEWELLYN ORDERING INFORMATION

Order online: Visit our website at www.llewellyn.com to select your books and place an order on our secure server.

Order by phone:
- • Call toll free within the U.S. at 1-877-NEW-WRLD (1-877-639-9753)
- • Call toll free within Canada at 1-866-NEW-WRLD (1-866-639-9753)
- • We accept VISA, MasterCard, and American Express

Order by mail:
Send the full price of your order (MN residents add 6.875% sales tax) in U.S. funds, plus postage and handling to: Llewellyn Worldwide, 2143 Wooddale Drive Woodbury, MN 55125-2989

POSTAGE AND HANDLING:

STANDARD: (U.S. & Canada)
(Please allow 2 business days)
$25.00 and under, add $4.00.
$25.01 and over, FREE SHIPPING.

INTERNATIONAL ORDERS (airmail only):
$16.00 for one book, plus $3.00 for each additional book.

Visit us online for more shipping options.
Prices subject to change.

FREE CATALOG!

To order, call
1-877-
NEW-WRLD
ext. 8236
or visit our
website

PARANORMAL OBSESSION
America's Fascination with
Ghosts & Hauntings, Spooks & Spirits
DEONNA KELLI SAYED

Paranormal Obsession

America's Fascination with Ghosts & Hauntings, Spooks & Spirits

DEONNA KELLI SAYED

Why is America so captivated by the unexplained? Far beyond a book of ghost stories, *Paranormal Obsession* offers a unique cultural studies approach to the global phenomena of spirits, ghost hunting, and all things otherworldly.

Providing an insider's view from within the spirit-seeking community, paranormal investigator Deonna Kelli Sayed explores how and why our love of spirits started, how ghosts took over the small screen, the roles of science and religion, our fascination with life after death—and what it all says about American culture.

Weighing perspectives of ghost hunters, religious figures, scientists, academics, parapsychologists, and cast members of the popular TV shows *Ghost Hunters* and *Paranormal State,* this book offers compelling insight into Americans' fixation on ghostly activity. It also highlights the author's paranormal group's investigation of the USS North Carolina, the most haunted battleship in the United States.

978-0-7387-2635-9, 264 pp., 6 x 9 $15.95

To order, call 1-877-NEW-WRLD
Prices subject to change without notice
Order at Llewellyn.com 24 hours a day, 7 days a week!

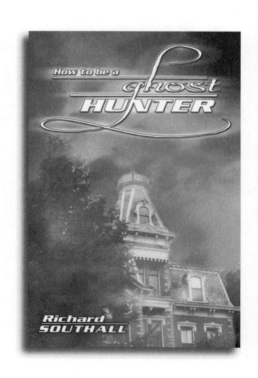

How To Be a Ghost Hunter
RICHARD SOUTHALL

So you want to investigate a haunting? This book is full of practical advice used in the author's own ghost-hunting practice. Find out whether you're dealing with a ghost, a spirit, or an entity... and discover the one time when you should stop what you're doing and call in an exorcist. Learn the four-phase procedure for conducting an effective investigation, how to capture paranormal phenomena on film, record disembodied sounds and voices on tape, assemble an affordable ghost-hunting kit, and form your own paranormal group.

For anyone with time and little money to spend on equipment, this book will help you maintain a healthy sense of skepticism and thoroughness while you search for authentic evidence of the paranormal.

978-0-7387-0312-1, 168 pp., 5³⁄₁₆ x 8   **$12.95**

Marcus F. Griffin

Foreword by Jeff Belanger

EXTREME PARANORMAL

INVESTIGATIONS

The Blood Farm Horror,
the Legend of Primrose Road,
and Other Disturbing Hauntings

Extreme Paranormal Investigations
The Blood Farm Horror, the Legend of Primrose Road, and Other Disturbing Hauntings
Marcus F. Griffin

Set foot inside the bone-chilling, dangerous, and sometimes downright terrifying world of extreme paranormal investigations. Join Marcus F. Griffin, Wiccan priest and founder of Witches in Search of the Paranormal (WISP), as he and his team explore the Midwest's most haunted properties. These investigations include the creepiest-of-the-creepy cases WISP has tackled over the years, many of them in locations that had never before been investigated. These true-case files include investigations of Okie Pinokie and the Demon Pillar Pigs, the Ghost Children of Munchkinland Cemetery, and the Legend of Primrose Road. Readers will also get an inside glimpse of previously inaccessible places, such as the former Jeffrey Dahmer property as WISP searches for the notorious serial killer's spirit, and the farm that belonged to Belle Gunness, America's first female serial killer and the perpetrator of the Blood Farm Horror.

978-0-7387-2697-7, 264 pp., 5³⁄₁₆ x 8 $15.95

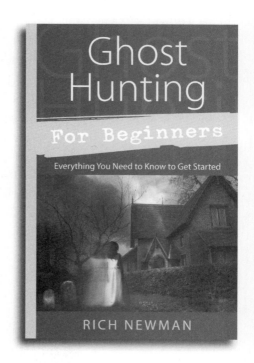

Ghost Hunting For Beginners
Everything You Need to Know to Get Started
Rich Newman

For the countless fans of ghost hunting TV shows who are itching to get off the couch and track some spirits on their own, professional ghost hunter Rich Newman arms beginners with all they need to start investigating.

Discover proven scientific methods and the latest technology used by the pros. You'll learn about what ghosts are, why hauntings occur, the different types of supernatural phenomena, conducting responsible investigations, forming a team, interacting with spirits, examining evidence—and what not to do when seeking spirits. Peppered with ghost stories from famous cases and the author's own investigations, this book will help you become a true paranormal investigator.

978-0-7387-2696-0, 240 pp., 5³⁄₁₆ x 8   **$14.95**

The Ghost Hunter's Field Guide
Over 1000 Haunted Places You Can Experience
RICH NEWMAN

Ghost hunting isn't just on television. More and more paranormal investigation groups are popping up across the nation. To get in on the action, you need to know where to go.

The Ghost Hunter's Field Guide features over a thousand haunted places around the country in all fifty states. Visit battlefields, theaters, saloons, hotels, museums, resorts, parks, and other sites teeming with ghostly activity. Each location—haunted by the spirits of murderers, Civil War soldiers, plantation slaves, and others—is absolutely safe and accessible.

This indispensable reference guide features over a hundred photos and offers valuable information for each location, including the tales behind the haunting and the kind of paranormal phenomena commonly experienced there: apparitions, shadow shapes, phantom aromas, telekinetic activity, and more.

978-0-7387-2088-3, 432 pp., 6 x 9   **$17.95**

MELBA GOODWYN
Chasing Graveyard Ghosts
INVESTIGATIONS OF HAUNTED AND HALLOWED GROUND

Chasing Graveyard Ghosts
Investigations of Haunted and Hallowed Ground
Melba Goodwyn

Angry ghosts, malevolent red-eyed orbs, graveyard statues that come to life... Take a spine-tingling tour of haunted graveyards, from an incredibly active vampire burial site to Voodoo Queen Marie Laveaux's wishing tomb.

Paranormal investigator Melba Goodwyn explores the ghostly phenomena, spooky legends, and frightful folklore associated with cemeteries. Fortified with her own hair-raising experiences, she offers insights into the graveyard ghosts and guardians, spirited statues, bizarre tombstone inscriptions, portals linking other dimensions, and ghost passageways along ley lines. There's also practical guidance for those who wish to investigate the many mysteries—paranormal and otherwise—that cemeteries hold.

978-0-7387-2126-2, 312 pp., 5³⁄₁₆ x 8   **$16.95**

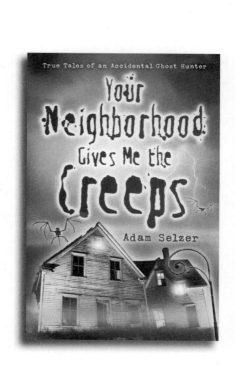

Your Neighborhood Gives Me the Creeps
True Tales of an Accidental Ghost Hunter
ADAM SELZER

Getting pushed down the stairs by unseen hands? An old spirit hag sitting on your chest, holding you down? Strange glowing ectoplasm escaping from a grave? Don't believe everything you hear … but then again, some things can't just be brushed off.

Come aboard the ghost bus and get a glimpse of Chicago's ghostly goings-on. With a healthy dose of skepticism, professional ghostbuster Adam Selzer takes you on a tour of his famously spooky town and the realm of the weird. Tag along with your tour guide Selzer, bus driver and improv comic Hector, psychic detective Ken, and prolific author Troy Taylor as they uncover cool evidence of the supernatural. Entertaining and thought-provoking, this book will make believers and skeptics alike want to tromp through their local cemetery to see if it's really haunted (or just dark and creepy).

978-0-7387-1557-5, 288 pp., 5³⁄₁₆ x 8   **$15.95**